THE ART OF BEING
UNREASONABLE

THE ART OF BEING
UNREASONABLE

LESSONS IN
UNCONVENTIONAL THINKING

ELI BROAD
WITH SWATI PANDEY

To Sam,

Eli Broad

WILEY

John Wiley & Sons Inc.

To Edye, the love of my life

CONTENTS

FOREWORD

Michael Bloomberg

W e have all met unreasonable people in our lives. Some of us have even been called unreasonable—or worse. But if ever there's been someone qualified to write a book on being unreasonable, it is Eli Broad. And if ever there's been a time when we need more people to be unreasonable—in business, philanthropy, and especially government—it's right now.

Eli Broad's life is a great American story, not only because it is a story of hard work and success, but because it's a story of dreams—of pushing into new frontiers and believing that the impossible can be achieved. That's what Eli has done throughout his life, and it's why he has accomplished as much as he has. But this book is less about what Eli has done and more about how he has done it.

I first met Eli some 30 years ago, back when I was just starting my own company. Eli had already built a Fortune 500 company from scratch, KB Home—and he would go on to build a second: SunAmerica. Maybe the second time is easier, but I doubt it. Building a company is an all-consuming undertaking that requires an enormous amount of dedication, an unflagging belief in your idea, and plenty of good luck. But to me, the fact that he built a second Fortune 500 company is less impressive than the fact that he set out to do it in the first place. Plenty of other people would have kicked back and enjoyed an early retirement. Not Eli. He wanted to continue building—and he had the guts to try to do it in an entirely different industry.

Within these pages, you will find a firsthand account of how he built those two Fortune 500 companies; how he helped shape Los Angeles into a cultural and architectural capital; how he is working to revolutionize the way we diagnose, treat, and prevent disease; and how he is helping transform public education around the nation, including in New York City.

When I was first elected mayor of New York in 2001, I set out to transform the city's broken and dysfunctional Board of Education and turn around a school system that had been failing students for decades. It was a daunting challenge; the New York City school system has 1.1 million students, which would make it the 10th largest city in the United States, just behind Dallas. Ending decades of dysfunction and replacing it with a culture of innovation and excellence would require bold action and a willingness to take on the special interests—and to do that, we knew we would need lots of support. We reached out to private sector leaders and philanthropists and asked them to become our partners—and Eli Broad was one of the very first calls we made.

Eli understands how important education reform is to the future of our country, and he is as passionate as I am about putting the needs of children first—no matter what the special interests say. Over the past decade, Eli has been instrumental in helping us undertake major reforms, including launching the NYC Leadership Academy to train the next generation of principals, creating more charter school options for students and parents, and strengthening accountability.

As a result, our students have made enormous progress, and today, high school graduation rates are 40 percent higher than they were when we began. When New York City won the prestigious Broad Prize for Urban Education in 2007, we could not have been more honored.

Eli and I both believe that philanthropy is most valuable—and powerful—when it dares to go where governments will not or cannot, and he has provided critical support in helping us launch promising but untested ideas. This willingness to take risks has been a defining characteristic of Eli's life. Yet he has been so successful not only because he is fearless and forward-looking but also because he does his homework. He studies the data, analyzes trends, and identifies opportunities that others may miss. Whether in business or philanthropy, he is an entrepreneur in everything he does—always open to new ideas, always looking for new approaches, and always willing to buck the conventional wisdom.

When Eli embraced the idea for a genomic medical research center that would bring together scientists from MIT and Harvard, he was told that the two rival universities would never collaborate on such a project. He ignored that advice, and today The Broad Institute is changing the way we understand science and medicine. Of course, Eli has also had his share of crazy ideas—like the time he wanted to buy the Tribune Company. Even though I own a media business, I told him he was out of his mind, and he came to agree that he was lucky to be the unsuccessful bidder.

The Eli Broad you will meet in these pages is the Eli Broad I've gotten to know and admire: honest and tough, blunt and direct. When he speaks and writes, he has no use for business jargon or management gibberish. His language is as clear as his vision. You will also meet the one person who is the secret of his success: his wife, Edye. She is truly a full partner in all that they do. And when Eli is unreasonable, Edye is gracious, kind, and understanding. Together, they are one talented team.

This book holds lessons for anyone who has ever failed—and anyone who has ever dreamt big. As someone who started a company after getting fired, I know how difficult it is to swim against the tide. When I first started a business making financial information more easily accessible via computers, everyone thought I was crazy. "That's not the way the industry works," I was told. And when I decided to run for mayor of New York, everyone thought I was *really* crazy. "You don't know the first thing about politics!" I was told. And that was true. But I knew what Eli knows: If you want to achieve the impossible, you have to start by being unreasonable.

Of course, being unreasonable can also be a recipe for disaster. So how do you learn the art of being unreasonable? Keep reading.

Michael Bloomberg is mayor of New York City, founder of Bloomberg LP, and an active philanthropist.

ACKNOWLEDGMENTS

Although I am solitary by nature, much of what I have been able to accomplish in each of my careers has been possible only because I always surround myself with a team of smart, hardworking, dedicated professionals. This book is no different, and although I offer up praise and appreciation sparingly, I would be remiss if I did not acknowledge the contributions that helped make this book a reality.

Special thanks to Swati Pandey, whose gift for prose transformed my thoughts and ideas into words better than I ever could have done alone. She is a talented young writer who I predict will have a long and prosperous future as a stunningly successful author. Quite simply, she was a joy to work with. Tim Rutten is a graceful wordsmith whose smart edits and wise counsel proved invaluable, and I appreciate his careful skill in refining the stories and lessons contained in these pages. Thank you to Karen Denne, my chief communications officer, for her exemplary coordination and invaluable qualitative oversight. Jim Newton's generous advice and keen eye for talent contributed to this project in ways too numerous to list. Thanks to Dan Wolf for helping get this book off the ground and for his continuing encouragement.

I was fortunate to have had a supportive and adept team at John Wiley & Sons, Inc. Senior editor Richard Narramore saw the potential of this book in its very early stages and helped shape it. Thanks to Lydia Dimitriadis, Lauren Freestone, Peter Knox, Chris Wallace, and Melissa Torra for their assistance shepherding us through the publishing process. Special thanks to my agent, Lisa Queen, for her support.

I have met a lot of people during my nearly 79 years. I am drawn to personalities different from my own, people who have a unique worldview and are accomplished in their varied fields. Over the years, Jeff Koons has become a dear friend. He generously allowed us to use the image of one of my favorite works of art, *Rabbit*, on the cover of this book, and for that I am grateful. Photographers Jay Clendenin and Nancy Pastor always make me look good, so I appreciate their talents. I have never met anyone like Eric Lander. You will read about him in these pages, and my only fear is that printed words could never do him justice. He is simply extraordinary, with passion, energy, and focus that are unmatched.

In our philanthropic work, my wife, Edye, and I are fortunate to be guided by a wise and credentialed board of governors, each of whom contributes a diverse perspective, informed by vast accomplishments. They help shape our philanthropic approach, which you will read about in the later chapters of this book.

The experiences expressed in these pages represent my best recollection, and any mistakes are unintended and solely my own. But I was aided in my memory by colleagues and friends Jay Wintrob, Jana Greer, Bruce Karatz, and Andrea Van de Kamp, who took time out of their busy schedules to help me recall many of the details I missed because I was moving too quickly to take note. I am fortunate to know them, and I treasure the times we shared, working together to build companies and institutions. And, Dick Riordan, I thank you for working with me on some of my most memorable undertakings and for our enduring friendship over nearly 40 years.

I have long admired Mike Bloomberg for his bold leadership, business acumen, and straight-shooter approach to life. He has become a valued friend, and I am delighted that he shared his thoughts in this book's foreword.

We have the very best team at The Broad Foundations, but there are a few people who deserve special mention. Gerun Riley is my chief of staff and right hand in virtually all of my endeavors. She is always one step ahead of me and juggles an extraordinary workload. She does it all with grace and superb skill. I am in capable and kind hands with Joane Ra and Kathleen Lungren Jobe, who keep me on track, always with the most gracious disposition. Edye and I are fortunate that Cindy Quane has overseen our family office for many years, and we are grateful for her loyalty. We have a whip-smart investment team. They advise me, challenge me, and always exhibit sharp insights. Thank you to Marc Schwartz and K.C. Krieger for their patience and persistence when I'm at my most unreasonable in matters of finance and investment. Their assistance with Chapter 12 helped me articulate what I often do instinctively.

The project that is consuming much of my attention these days is the construction of The Broad, our new museum in downtown Los Angeles. Despite the daunting amount of work that is filling their days and nights, Joanne Heyler and Deborah Kanter found time to contribute their insights to these pages. I am indebted to them for their continuing commitment to our work. There are many more members of our foundation team, too many to list individually but I have to express appreciation to Rachel Smookler, Gregory McGinity, Erica Lepping, Jeannine Guido, Molly Ryan, Hilary Rowe, and Tara McBride for their help with this book.

Three people have been a constant in much of my life, and I don't express my profound love for them often enough. To our sons, Jeffrey and Gary, I know I wasn't the easiest father. While I have been a demanding boss and businessman, I was also an impatient and exacting parent. Now, with the benefit of hindsight, I wish I had more time to make amends. But I offer you my love as deeply as a parent can.

Until my last day, I will count my blessings that Edythe Lawson agreed to become Edythe Broad. In recent years, I have referred to Edye as my chief inspiration officer. While others have tolerated me, Edye has loved me, unconditionally. She has stuck by me, covered my shortcomings, and brought a warmth and graciousness to our family and our friends that are unmatched. While I welcomed public interest and attention throughout my careers, Edye was enormously private and always shied away from crowds and cameras. Across the years, she accompanied me to most every dinner, gala, and gathering—often tucking off in a corner of a packed room with a book. Although Edye is a voracious reader—I've always joked that she is the largest book buyer on the West Coast—she didn't want me to write a book because she preferred to keep our lives private. But she proved to be my most valued editor and has always been my most treasured confidante. One of the best things about this book is the chance to tell the world how much she means to me. Edye, I love you.

Chapter 1

THE ART OF BEING UNREASONABLE

I am unreasonable.

It's the one adjective everyone I know—family, friends, associates, employees, and critics—has used to describe me.

Occasionally, some of them have also called me crazy or nuts. But they've all told me at some point that I was being unreasonable because my goals were unrealistic, my deadlines couldn't be met, my ideas were far-fetched, or my approach trampled on the conventional wisdom.

But I believe that being unreasonable has been the key to my success. In this book I want to show you how applying unreasonable thinking can help you achieve goals others may tell you are out of reach, just as it has for me.

Over the past six decades I have had four careers: accounting, homebuilding, retirement savings, and philanthropy. I became the first person to build two Fortune 500 companies from the ground up in two different industries. The $6 billion I earned in business is now being used to help reform public education in America, assemble two world-class art collections and make them widely accessible, and provide critical start-up funding for cutting-edge biomedical research.

What gives me the most satisfaction is that all my careers have demanded that I meet people's essential needs—helping them realize their dreams of homeownership and a secure retirement, educating their children, experiencing great art, and living a healthier life. Each has also required me to be quite unreasonable—to have outsized ambition,

1

discipline, energy, and focus and to have the confidence to ignore people who said I couldn't do it. If this book does nothing else, I hope it helps you silence the voice of conventional wisdom that too often keeps people from even attempting to achieve their goals.

Through my careers there has been one constant: a paperweight on my desk, a gift my wife, Edye, gave me some time after we were married in 1954. It sat on the tiny desk in a shared office in Detroit, Michigan, where, as a young CPA, I first envisioned starting the local homebuilding business that would become KB Home. It made the trip to Los Angeles, where it rested in my new office with a view of the Pacific Ocean at my retirement savings company, SunAmerica. Today, Edye's gift sits on the pale wood desk where I oversee The Broad Foundations' wide-ranging philanthropies. My office walls may be covered with art by Jasper Johns and photographs of the interesting people I have met during my career, but time and again—as it has so often over the years—my gaze goes to Edye's paperweight and its inscription, a quote from George Bernard Shaw: "The reasonable man adapts himself to the world. The unreasonable one persists in trying to adapt the world to himself. Therefore, all progress depends upon the unreasonable man."

You could say Edye and I got married because I was unreasonable. After a friend gave me Edye's phone number, I called out of the blue and asked her to dinner. She had no idea who I was and couldn't even remember my friend. She said yes only because her mother pressured her into it. I drove to her house one Saturday night and hoped that she wouldn't slam the door after seeing my big ears and goofy grin. Lucky for me, she didn't. Only a few dates later I proposed, promising her my vision of a great future: our own home, two kids, two cars, and maybe a vacation once a year to Florida.

Edye's yes was my greatest piece of good fortune. Our marriage remains Exhibit A in my case for the value of being unreasonable. In love and in business, if you know what you want, you have to go for it.

BEING UNREASONABLY UNREASONABLE

I didn't stop being unreasonable once Edye and I were married. Sometimes it made me harder to live with than I needed to be. I hadn't yet realized that there's an art to being effectively unreasonable. One night, for example, when Edye wanted to see a movie, I drove to the theater only to turn right back around when I saw the long line. I wasn't about to waste time standing around for tickets, even if, as Edye sensibly pointed out, there was no other way to see a movie.

A few months later, when we had barely settled into married life, I convinced her to sell our wedding china so that we could use the money to buy land. Edye was the only woman among her friends—maybe the only woman ever—who traded dishes for dirt.

Home wasn't the only place I was unreasonable. I didn't try too hard to hold on to my job at a small local accounting firm. I passed the CPA exam at age 20 on the first try—a test that took my boss and other higher-ups several tries to ace. As the youngest CPA in Michigan's history, I started demanding a raise. My boss didn't like that—or my refusal to drop the subject—and I was fired.

Asking your new boss for a raise because you did something he couldn't do is an example of being artlessly unreasonable. It's not a habit you want to cultivate because, frankly, it's just another way of being willful or selfish. It won't get you anywhere but into trouble.

After getting fired, I hung out the shingle of my own accounting firm. I found a rent-free office thanks to Edye's cousin's husband, Donald Kaufman, who let me share his. Don was a homebuilder who put up several houses a year and worked the rest of the time as a subcontractor on building sites. In exchange for the office, I told Don I would do his accounting.

Within several weeks of settling in, I was bored and restless. I had a few clients and I was teaching night courses in accounting at the Detroit Institute of Technology, but I still didn't have enough work to keep me busy. I wanted more money and more excitement.

The problem was the only thing I knew how to do was accounting. I wasn't interested in going into another line of work that required new credentials because I didn't want to go back to school. I had pushed myself hard to graduate cum laude from Michigan State University in just three years. I tried to get a job working at a home-builder but was turned away for lack of experience. That's when I asked myself, "Why not start my own homebuilding company?"

I thought about my skills and my personality and whether they would be a good fit for the field. I read industry magazines that I got at the library. Meticulous research, as you will see, became a key to my success in all four of my careers. I studied other homebuilders, who struck me as too inefficient and not focused enough on the best available financing. They could build a house blindfolded, but they didn't pay enough attention to their finances. A keen eye for numbers would be my competitive advantage.

I read and analyzed enough news to know that America in those years was moving from a nation of tenants to a country of homeowners. Building houses was not complicated, and I wasn't going to have to build them anyway. I would just have to manage subcontractors and suppliers and find a partner who knew his way around the field—which is exactly what Don Kaufman was. That's how we became Kaufman and Broad.

I told Edye my plans, and—instead of telling me I was nuts—she encouraged me to go for it. She also gave me the suggestion that made it all possible. She said to ask her dad, Morris, for start-up capital, $12,500. He said yes, and my first company was born.

Discovering the Art of Unreason

I heard complaints about how unreasonable I was as soon as I set foot on our first construction site. Some of my subcontractors owned shirts older than I was, and they weren't too keen on listening to me explain how they could build homes faster and more cheaply if they would just stick to the budget and schedule I had drawn up. But by then I had carefully researched the cost of all the material we would need and the time it would take to complete every step in the building process.

That alone wasn't enough to convince the contractors to work for us. Instead, I appealed to their interests. It was a little intimidating—I was a young kid asking seasoned contractors to work for less and wait a little longer to get paid. But they quickly saw my logic. If they stuck to my plan, our company would grow rapidly and they would have more work—even during the winter months, when building traditionally slows down. They took a chance with us, and the gamble paid off. We built 120 homes that first year. We made money—and so did our contractors.

Something similar happened three decades later, when I turned a small, rather sleepy insurance firm into the multibillion-dollar retirement savings company SunAmerica. Not long after the company spun off from Kaufman and Broad and became a separate publicly traded company in 1989, I walked into our conference room and told my senior executives that I wanted 20 percent growth every year. Again, there were murmurs from some of the more experienced hands that I was nuts.

But I had done my homework. Research—and using what you learn from it to analyze every situation—is what separates being unreasonable from being irrational. I knew we could achieve that high growth rate by acquiring smaller companies, building a broker network as big as Merrill Lynch's, and being the best at marketing and addressing customer needs. I promised my employees great rewards if they joined me in reaching for that unreasonable goal. When we got down to work, we turned SunAmerica into a provider of secure retirements for millions of Americans—and the best performing stock on the New York Stock Exchange from 1990 until we merged with American International Group (AIG) in 1998.

The world of philanthropy is no less suspicious of unreasonable ideas and goals. I heard the usual complaints whenever I tried anything ambitious: helping to launch the Museum of Contemporary Art in 1979, raising the money to build Los Angeles's acclaimed Walt Disney Concert Hall, working to transform K–12 urban school districts across America, and funding critical biomedical research with strategic investments in the style of a venture capitalist. All of those efforts succeeded, and I found that people who started out calling me crazy were suddenly happy to be my partners.

Victory, as the old saying goes, has many fathers. People will flock to support you when you do well, but in the crucial early moments, and whenever you try to create something out of nothing, you will be on a solitary path blocked by obstacles and doubt. If you're already on that kind of course, this book will speak to you in a special way. It will give you examples from my experience that will help you enlist allies and collaborators. It will show you how to smooth your unreason-ableness into an artful and focused drive. Being artfully unreasonable won't necessarily make you a good team player, but it can make you a dramatically effective leader.

If, instead, you worry a lot about what other people think and you fear being called unreasonable, this book will show you that with research, good analysis, and focus you can have the confidence to do what others would dismiss as unreasonable and achieve the successes nobody thought you could reach.

The lessons I've taken to heart from nearly 60 years in business and philanthropy are ones I still use every day: ask a lot of questions, pursue the untried, revise expectations upward, take risks, be restless, and most important, seek out the best in your work—the best deal, the best investment, the best people, the best causes, the best art—and the best in yourself.

Chapter 2

Why Not? The Powerful Question

If you've never heard my name pronounced, you probably think it rhymes with *rod*.

When my father immigrated to the United States, he added the *a* to his Lithuanian surname, Brod. He thought the extra vowel would make Brod seem less strange. Unfortunately, neither he nor the rest of his family—who happily adopted the new spelling and *rod* pronunciation—could foresee just how much fun the guys in my junior high school would have calling me "broad."

Then I had an idea: Why not change my name?

Broad, however, was my family's name. It was the name on the sign above the Detroit five-and-dime my father owned. Legally changing my name would also involve a trip to court, which would trigger more ridicule when the other kids found out I had done something so drastic just to avoid teasing. So, I thought, why not alter just the pronunciation? "Broad, rhymes with road," I started telling people, from teachers on down to my classmates. I told my parents about the switch one evening at dinner. They just smiled and shook their heads. They knew even then that there wasn't a lot they could do to change my mind—and I learned the advantage of reframing the facts in a way nobody had considered before.

The name stuck. I became "Eli Broad, rhymes with road." Some of the teasing continued, but it didn't really sting anymore. I had changed myself. I liked my new name. To me it seemed strong and refined. I still say, "Rhymes with road," when I introduce myself to people for the first time, and I'm still happy with the way it sounds. I even enjoy the association with the word *road,* which always suggests a way forward—my preferred direction.

It all started just because I asked a simple question: "Why not?"

"Why Not?" as the First Step to Success

Children instinctively ask, "Why not?" Adults soon lose the habit, in large part because they have accepted the status quo. But that's exactly when you need to ask the question with greater force. The questions you're willing to ask when others think they have all the answers are doors to discovery.

Asking "Why not?" worked for my parents. Both were Jewish immigrants from Lithuania. My mom's family was in the timber business back home and had some money, but my father had nothing in the old country and even less when he arrived in New York. They often needed extra money, so they decided to open, of all things, a Christmas store. They had no experience, they had never run a store, and they were Jewish—but why not? They rented an empty storefront for two months every year. I helped them stock shelves and sell cards, strings of lights, stockings, wrapping paper, and last-minute gifts. My parents worked long hours right up until Christmas Eve, when everyone else was with their families. All of a sudden, what started as a strange idea—one the conventional wisdom said my parents had no business pursuing— became a major part of getting our family through the Great Depression.

My first business also began with "Why not?" when I was 13 years old. I had been collecting stamps since I was 5, living in a walk-up apartment in the Bronx with my parents. My Uncle Misha lived upstate in Peekskill and collected stamps from around the world. I often spent weekends at his house, flipping through his grand old leather volumes of stamps—learning how to pick out the good ones, how to store them properly, how much they were worth. I continued collecting even after we moved to Detroit when I was 7 years old. I bought stamps whenever I had some spare money, getting sheets of them at the post office the first day a new set came out. I started reading stamp collecting magazines and spent weekends riding the streetcar to downtown Detroit, where stamp dealers would set up shop in empty storefronts. I once discovered an early American stamp on the floor at a convention. (I suppose it helped that, at my age, I was the closest to the floor and shyly looking down.) It was more valuable than any other stamp I owned.

I loved the atmosphere around the weekend stamp dealers— trading, haggling, looking for that perfect find. It was my first taste of the excitement I would come to love in the business world, the constant urge to do more and better. I decided I wanted to experience that rush as a seller and not just as a casual buyer.

As a 13-year-old, though, operating out of a storefront was out of the question. Then, one weekend, I saw an ad in one of the collectors' magazines. Chrysler International, the auto company, was selling boxes of stamps that had been clipped off the envelopes it received from around the world. Each box weighed 2 pounds and cost a few dollars. Although I was already good with numbers, I couldn't quite calculate how many stamps that would be for a very low price, but I knew the figure was significant.

That was the moment I had to ask, "Why not?" I could already imagine the obstacles and objections I'd have to overcome: the office workers at Chrysler asking me what the heck I was doing wandering around their headquarters, my parents asking why I needed to go to the offices of one of the Big Three automakers, and other stamp collectors just not wanting to do business with a kid. But there was no really good reason why not, why it couldn't be me, as long as I had the idea and the money—and the follow-through.

I took the streetcar by myself to Chrysler. I walked through the lobby, pretending I was meant to be there. I asked the first adult I saw for directions to the mailroom, where my stamps awaited. Once I found my way, I handed a man two crumpled dollar bills and took the box. No one gave me the slightest trouble.

I went home and put some ads in magazines, advertising a hundred stamps for $1.95. Orders came in from around the country—a bunch of checks made out to me. Everyone assumed I was a grown-up with a bank account. I made more than $10 off my $2 investment in that first box. The money was so good that I stopped saving for more stamps and started saving for a car, although I was still too young to drive. When I was 16, I bought a 1941 Chevy for $200. It was old and beaten up and the tires were worn. But it ran. It was the ride that stamps bought.

Nothing Sets Me Off More Than Being Told I Can't Do Something

Too often, age and experience become an excuse for accepting the status quo without question. Instead of asking "Why not?" you become overwhelmed with all the reasons something can't be done. "Of course not" becomes your automatic response. You grow fearful of making mistakes. You rely on conventional wisdom because that's what everyone else does, and there's safety in consensus.

I fell into that trap when my high school teachers made it very clear to me that they found my constant questions annoying. Without answers or encouragement, I stopped asking—and stopped paying attention in class. I threw myself into my after-school jobs, such as selling women's shoes, and my grades fell. As graduation approached, I applied only to Michigan colleges and decided to pursue a pre-law major. It just seemed like the thing to do. I had let myself slip into autopilot, just going along.

Michigan State University (at the time it was Michigan State College) changed all that—and taught me vital lessons beyond the classroom. When "Why not?" disappears from our vocabulary, we often need something to jar us—inspiration from teachers or friends, new places, new challenges.

What first kicked me out of my stupor was a rule I didn't like. Michigan State prohibited drinking beer in the dorms. I didn't care that much about beer. It was the restriction that rubbed me the wrong way—and besides, I hated the dorm food. I could have done what many others did and just eaten off campus and broken the rule on beer. That, however, would have put my status as a student at risk. I wasn't willing to do that. My parents hadn't gone to college, and I wanted to get a degree, for me and for them. So instead, I thought, why not just live where I could do what I wanted?

Moving out of the dorms wouldn't be easy, I knew, because freshmen were supposed to live on campus. Getting to and from campus would be an additional burden. In any event, I told the school a little white lie—that I was living at home and commuting from Detroit—and moved into the local YMCA. It was brand-new, and I'd never lived anywhere brand-new. More to the point, I could eat and drink whatever I liked.

Not long after the move, I discovered I liked college. My professors appreciated questions, so I started asking them again. In 1952, during my sophomore year, I had a particularly fine economics instructor, Walter Adams, who would later become president of Michigan State University and write many books. He was only 11 years older than I was, and he could hold the attention of a bunch of teenagers like nobody I'd ever seen. He taught us from future Nobel Laureate Paul Samuelson's famous economics textbook. He also had us read what would become one of my favorite books, *Beckoning Frontiers: Public and Personal Recollections,* the memoirs of Marriner S. Eccles, who was President Franklin D. Roosevelt's choice for chairman of the Federal Reserve Bank.

I credit Professor Adams with interesting me in accounting. It was a perfect field for me because I was good with numbers. I was—even then—a pragmatist and couldn't envision a future in the esoteric pursuit of higher mathematics or theoretical economics. If I switched from pre-law to accounting, I could finish school early, get right to work, and maybe even eventually own my own store like my parents. "Why not?" I thought, as Professor Adams inspired me to make one of the most important choices of my life. That was the moment when asking "Why not?" became a lifelong habit.

"Why Not?" Should Be Something You Ask Every Day

Big decisions shouldn't be the only ones you reach by asking "Why not?" If you can make that question part of your routine thinking, you will find unexpected and beneficial ways to improve the status quo.

Before Kaufman and Broad went public, for example, I decided I wanted to employ the best accounting firm and I wanted first crack at its attention. My background made me a stickler for smart accounting, which is much more than totaling columns of figures. Rather than bumping elbows at the end of every calendar year with all the other companies trying to close their books, I simply asked, "Why not move the end of our fiscal year?"

Most firms close their fiscal year on either December 31 or June 30 or the last day of another quarter. We simply decided to end our year on November 30, which allowed us to hire the best accountants at the best rates and without a hint of the burnout that comes from working the financials of so many companies at once. To this day, more than 20 years after I stopped running the company, KB Home's financial year ends on November 30. Anyone, in any line of work, can use "Why not?" to make this kind of relatively small but significant change in day-to-day operations.

"Why not?" also helps me navigate options—weeding out the foolish while not shying away from the challenging. It's a question that helps sharpen my convictions and break down my unexamined prejudices. Over the years, it has become something of a personal mantra. When doubts assail me at crucial moments, I remind myself of all the things informed opinion told me I couldn't do but that I went on to accomplish. Then I ask myself, "Why not prove 'em wrong again?"

I suspect my inclination to ask "Why not?" was planted during what was, in many ways, a solitary childhood in which there were few adults to tell me no. Perhaps it also came from a childhood experience that I remember profoundly: Visiting the 1939 New York World's Fair right before my family moved from the Bronx to Detroit. I recall we paid a little more than a dollar to get in. I saw whole planned cities and towns. I saw my first fax machine and my first television set, which I watched for a long time, totally spellbound, even though the only things on the screen were images of people walking right by me. I could have just turned around. But that screen, that box, and every other object of realized imagination at that wonderful fair had begun, I instinctively knew, with a "Why not?"

One of Robert Kennedy's favorite quotations, like the inscription on my paperweight, was from George Bernard Shaw: "Some people see things as they are and say, why? I dream things that never were and say, why not?"

One of the things you'll discover when you ask "Why not?" is that life is richer when you live it among the dreamers.

Chapter 3

FORGET CONVENTIONAL WISDOM

When you have done the unreasonable thing, which is what most people call thinking for yourself, and asked the forbidden question "Why not?" you've empowered yourself with conventional wisdom's polar opposite: unconventional insight. That's the quality you always need to start a business, take a risk, or make any major decision.

Economically and personally, there couldn't have been a worse time to start a new business than 1956, the year I launched what ultimately became a Fortune 500 company. The first major downturn of the postwar era—the so-called Eisenhower recession—was about to start, and the homebuilding market was already jittery. Edye and I were expecting our first child. We had a mortgage. I had lost my $67.40-a-week accounting job, and we were living on my income from a few accounting clients and the night classes I was teaching at the Detroit Institute of Technology.

Actually, I liked both teaching and accounting, but my meager earnings weren't quite enough to give Edye the life I had promised. All I could see when I looked at the years ahead was more of the same, and that was not the future I wanted. As everyone else trimmed their expectations and ambitions to fit the nation's prevailing pessimism, I ignored the conventional wisdom and came to the unreasonable conclusion that even recessions can yield opportunity.

CONVENTIONAL WISDOM STRANGLES INNOVATION

Reasonable people treat conventional wisdom with respect. Those of us who are unreasonable regard it as an expression of the herd instinct. It's a fine quality for sheep—creatures that usually end up getting sheared—but not for entrepreneurs.

Most successful businesses have to begin by bucking conventional wisdom. Invention and innovation don't happen without it. Someone certainly told Jeff Bezos of Amazon.com that no one would buy a book without picking it up and looking at it in a store. People probably told Ted Turner when he was starting CNN that no one would want to watch—let alone advertise on—a 24-hour news channel.

The first bit of conventional wisdom that my homebuilding partner, Don Kaufman, and I encountered was the firm belief that no one in Detroit would buy a house without a basement. We asked, "Why not?" The answer produced our first big idea: no basements.

From reading industry magazines, I already knew that home-builders in Indianapolis, Indiana, and Dayton, Ohio, were building houses without basements and families were buying them. Basements had historically been the place to store coal to heat your home for the winter. New gas heating eliminated the need to stockpile coal, so basements weren't a necessity. If we skipped building them, we could put up homes faster and sell them for less than our competitors. We also could price our houses for first-time buyers, who I figured wouldn't move out of their apartments unless mortgage payments were less than their rent.

We constructed two basement-less model homes and bought options on 15 more lots. We also made a few other departures from convention to build a better-priced product. We used a combination of wood and brick facing rather than the more expensive all-brick fronts that were popular at the time. There were no architects' fees because I designed the floor plan myself. I made sure that there was as little hall space as possible, which meant bigger living areas. We threw in a carport, a nice perk at a time when many families in Detroit still parked on the street.

I carefully studied every step that went into putting up a home, and by scrutinizing every expense and eliminating all the nonessentials,

I came up with a no-frills house that could be constructed on an accelerated schedule. Less time with guys standing around on the job site and no wasted materials created instant advantages for our company.

Unconventional economies allowed us to set our price at $13,740, which was a full $2,000 less than the closest competition. That translated into a monthly payment of around $65, depending on the down payment. If the buyer was a veteran, as many in those days were, a down payment wasn't even needed. Don and I papered the city with flyers advertising our bare-bones, unfurnished models, which I christened "The Award Winner." Thankfully, nobody ever asked what prize we had won.

The weekend our models opened, I wanted to be anywhere but in Detroit. Everyone was throwing shovelfuls of the conventional wisdom at us: Nobody would buy a house without a basement, and even if they did, we would go broke trying to sell houses at such a low price. We were confident, but we were a little nervous too. So Edye; Don; his wife, Glorya; and I drove to Dayton, Ohio, for the weekend. We looked at a few model houses, just to compare notes, and had a steak dinner. We started the drive back to Detroit on Sunday. Halfway there, I couldn't wait any longer to find out how we had done. I pulled off the road, walked into a diner, went straight to the pay phone, and dialed our sales rep. He gave me the incredible news: We had sold 15 houses, all the lots we had, with sales of more than $200,000.

In our first year of business, we sold 120 houses, generating $1.7 million in revenue for our new company. That was a long way from scraping by as a $67.40-a-week accountant. I had enough money to pay back my father-in-law, and a few years later, I treated myself to a new car, a Thunderbird convertible. To build that beauty, Ford had bucked the conventional wisdom too. No one thought anyone would buy a two-seater that looked like a sports car but didn't have the engine to qualify—the Thunderbird was just a standard chassis dressed up in a fancy new suit. But Ford went with it. They called it a "personal luxury car" and that's precisely what it felt like to me.

Innovation Is a Permanent Revolution

Conventional wisdom abhors innovation. It's never a good time to change—far better to return to your company's fundamentals, or to focus on the next quarter's revenue, or just to continue doing what you do best. That may sound wise, but it's a recipe for stagnation. Consider the examples of the companies I mentioned earlier. Amazon.com discovered that along with books, customers would buy most any imaginable product online. CNN launched its news website in 1995, and it is now the most popular news site on the Web—and my source during the day for news of the financial markets. Successful companies innovate constantly—the products they offer, how they sell them, or how they conduct operations. Whether you're starting a business or launching a nonprofit or civic initiative, now is the time to innovate.

If Kaufman and Broad had remained simply a company that built homes without basements, someone else would have come along and done it better. We knew we had to come up with our next move soon after we sold those first 15 houses.

We started by looking at some of the industry's most fundamental operating principles, what most people would call the basics. They represent the strongest, stickiest—and most unexamined—kind of conventional wisdom. Often they've gone so long without scrutiny that they're accepted as gospel. That's what makes these core assumptions the best place to look for opportunities to innovate, no matter what business you're in.

One of the things I quickly noticed was that, although our competitors called themselves homebuilders, they really thought they were in the real estate business. Obviously, a builder needs land, which you sell right along with the house. For homebuilders who saw themselves as being in real estate, it made sense to buy a lot of land and hold on to it, treating it as inventory to be drawn down as needed. But by holding on to inventory, you're also tying up cash that could be put to work elsewhere.

So we changed the basics of our business. Instead of thinking of Kaufman and Broad as a real estate business, I decided we were manufacturers. We made and sold a product—a house. Back then, only the biggest homebuilders, like Bill Levitt, had the scale and capital to truly operate as manufacturers. But I studied their methods and figured out a way to do it at Kaufman and Broad despite our smaller size. We would treat land as just another raw material, like lumber or nails. We would buy it when we needed it and let someone else own it when we didn't.

Once we saw ourselves as manufacturers, we also kept watch over every bit of material we used. This was not a typical practice among our competitors in Detroit. Our contractors were used to allowing a lot of materials to go to waste. Don and I would stalk our construction sites, pointing out every scrap and adjusting our orders until we knew pretty much down to the last bolt, brick, and two-by-four what it took to build a house. That's all we paid for, nothing more. That attention to even the smallest expense has remained with me throughout my career, no matter that the numbers are bigger.

Along with keeping costs low, we had to make sure our financing wasn't expensive. We had to avoid taking out costly construction loans like most homebuilders did to cover building expenses. I realized we could pay contractors and suppliers from the money we received when the house was built and the sale closed. That meant we had to build a house within 45 days, which was four weeks faster than our closest competition. Then we could pay the contractors by the end of the month following the completion of their work. Bills came due, depending on when we completed a house, between 31 and 60 days after the work was done. The money flow would average out without us having to draw on expensive borrowed cash.

The schedule worked. Our cash flow from closings covered our bills—something that was unheard of in the homebuilding business.

My accounting background and my focus on the bottom line helped us continue to innovate financially. We developed a reputation among banks and investors for doing what no other homebuilder had ever done: gaining access to unsecured credit and eventually issuing our own commercial paper, both of which enabled us to reduce costs. We even launched our own mortgage company so customers could more easily arrange financing when they bought one of our houses. That venture was so successful that we started selling mortgages to other homebuilders' customers.

Success Is a Starting Point, Not a Conclusion

Changing the basics of our business helped Kaufman and Broad lay a foundation for growth. We grew faster than anyone expected, including ourselves. We looked around, saw we had the capital and the organizational culture to play in a bigger league, and thought, "Why not?"

We expanded first to Arizona and then to California, a market dominated by bigger and more experienced builders who knew how to maneuver within complex regulatory and political structures. To beat the big guys we knew we would have to come out of the starting gate with something new. This time our innovation was a contemporary version of the traditional East Coast row house. We would build in what was then a middle-class beachside community in Orange County called Huntington Beach.

Much like Midwestern houses without basements, no one thought row houses would work in the West, which was, in those days at least, all about space and sprawl. But I thought they made great sense. Everyone in Southern California wanted to live by the coast, but fewer and fewer could afford it. We designed smaller homes that shared one or two walls, making them less costly than stand-alone structures. We made sure they had distinct façades to give each house a unique appearance. We added a community clubhouse with a pool for all the homeowners to share, an added perk to make up for the lost square footage and side yards.

We called them "townhouses." Today they're a staple of the housing market throughout Southern California. We sold our first 756 Huntington Continental Townhouses in five weeks.

I did make one rookie mistake. We should have sold 50 at one price and then raised prices. Step pricing might have slowed sales, but it would have been financially smarter. We could have covered any unexpected changes in our materials and labor costs while boosting our profits. Pricing can be a big tripping point for a new business, especially because it can seem as if the only way into a market is to slash the price and make it up in volume. We stuck to our pricing strategy too long. We set the price according to our costs, which we kept low.

NOTHING LASTS FOREVER

When you're on a winning streak, it's easy to think it will last forever. It won't. It never does.

By 1971 Kaufman and Broad was Wall Street's darling. We went public on the American Stock Exchange in 1961 and became the first homebuilder listed on the New York Stock Exchange in 1969. We had almost single-handedly taken our industry out of an era of private ownership—when investors regarded homebuilders as unstable and poorly managed, liable to go bust in any down market. We had convinced analysts that a well-run housing company was immune to the ups and downs of the business cycle. Most stock pickers thought homebuilding would boom in the 1970s.

But I wasn't totally convinced myself. It's important to pay attention to the lessons of history and know the realities of your industry. In other words, don't believe the conventional wisdom you create about yourself.

So while investors bid up Kaufman and Broad's stock, we bought a small life insurance company to help stabilize earnings during downturns in the housing market. The biggest housing slump since the

Great Depression hit three years later, and that acquisition, Sun Life Insurance Company of America, pulled us through.

Look Outside Your Personal and Professional Comfort Zone

Sun Life was an old-line insurance company based in Baltimore, Maryland, and when we bought it in 1971, it operated much the same way it did when it was founded in 1890. It had a history of modest growth, no better or worse than most other insurers. The company focused on the basics of the insurance business: taking in premiums, holding on to them, and making sure there was enough in the bank to pay claims. They kept their cash from premiums in traditional, low-return investments.

About eight years after we acquired the company, I looked at the industry to see where we might find a niche. Other insurers—most of them bigger and better known—were introducing new kinds of life insurance policies. I figured they would do well selling those products, and we would just lag behind if we tried the same. Instead, I pushed Sun Life away from life insurance and toward retirement savings. Our customers would be the same baby boomers who purchased Kaufman and Broad's houses: a big generation of spenders who would live long past retirement age and, therefore, would be thinking more about retirement than death. That's when I thought to introduce fixed and variable annuities—which actually were mutual funds in life insurance wrappers.

With variable annuities, we made money on fees while the policyholder decided how to invest and received the returns from and assumed the risks of their investment. With fixed annuities, we promised a particular rate of return while handling the investment and risk ourselves. We made our profit on the "spread"—the difference between what we ultimately paid out and what we could earn from investing the premiums.

Profiting from the spread required changing the basics of the business, as we had done with Kaufman and Broad. We decided that instead of thinking like an insurer, we should think like a bank. What banks do is pretty simple: They buy money at one price, and sell it at another; that is, banks take in deposits and promise to pay you interest at a given rate. Then they loan money out at a higher rate, and the difference between your interest rate and the borrower's is profit. I decided we would adopt a banking mentality at Sun Life. We promised a certain rate of return to our customers on their policies, and we would earn a higher rate of return from our investments.

We changed the name of our company in 1993 to SunAmerica, in part to reflect that we were a new type of company, not a plain old insurer. We focused our energies on our investments, which began to grow at a faster rate than other insurers', and earned 2 to 3 percent more a year than our competitors. That sort of performance enabled us to do even more for our customers, such as introducing new products and promising better returns.

Kaufman and Broad and SunAmerica both prospered beyond all expectation because I was unreasonable enough to ask fundamental questions about unexamined assumptions. We came up with ways to reimagine our businesses. A real estate company became a manufacturer and a life insurer became a bank. Both became Fortune 500 companies. That's the value of unconventional insight.

Chapter 4

Do Your Homework No Matter How Much Time It Takes

When I was a kid, my father would occasionally go to the horse races. Sometimes he took me with him, and I watched him lose a few hard-earned dollars from his five-and-dime.

Neither he nor my mom was very happy when I started hanging around the track as a college student. But I thought I could make the ponies my route to a quick buck.

That part of the plan didn't work out, of course, but I learned some valuable lessons about shortcuts.

I've always had a good head for numbers, and for a while I relied on that to get me by. I would look at the odds and go over the horse's workout times and recent races. I would roughly balance what I hoped to win against how much risk I was willing to take. (It was usually the same then as it is today: a lot.) Some days I would win, and some days I wouldn't.

Then I thought, why not put a little more work into this? I started to follow the trainers around, taking notes and asking all kinds of pesky questions. Usually they answered, even if they would eventually shoo me away. My bets got a lot smarter, which meant I made some money.

Soon I gave up horses for stocks. That's when my effort—my homework—really started to pay off. If you spend all your time looking for shortcuts instead of doing what you have to do, you may never reach your goal. But do your homework and put in the necessary effort, and you'll reap the rewards.

Don't Waste Time on Shortcuts—They're Usually Dead Ends

Nearly all "get rich quick" schemes are pure bunk, but every year lots of people are seduced by them. That's why television shows promising millions of dollars in prizes attract lines of contestants. It's why a man named Charles Ponzi became infamous and why people continued to invest with Bernie Madoff when common sense should have told them those returns couldn't be real.

I'm always amused watching movies about people who achieve some big success because often the critical ingredient to their success— the long periods of hard work—is condensed into moments overlaid with catchy music. If there ever was a film version of my life, that montage surely would be my company's transformation of a small insurance company into a major player in retirement savings. We bought Sun Life Insurance Company in 1971 for $52 million and sold it, as the retirement savings company SunAmerica, for $18 billion in 1998. The intervening 27 years were filled with hard work—most of it directed toward an end I couldn't see but one I hoped would be profitable.

I had been prepared for that sort of marathon effort by personal experience. When I was a kid, I had fought a lonely struggle with a problem whose name—dyslexia—I wouldn't learn until doctors diagnosed our son with it decades later. As a boy, all I knew was that it was hard for me to read, and there was no way around that except to read a lot, and slowly, until I got the hang of it. It wasn't easy. But I got to the point that, as an adult, I could read—and enjoy—four newspapers each morning before work.

Pay Attention to History

I read not only to stay informed but also to get ideas. I read about what other companies are up to, what my peers are doing, where and when the next investment opportunity might be. Whether you're buying a company, considering changing jobs, or undertaking any serious project, you have to start by doing your homework. It's important to spend some of your day, every day, learning about the present and the past. Learn from others' successes and mistakes. History is scattered with clues to the future, but you won't find them if you don't look.

At Kaufman and Broad, we saw that the economy of the 1960s was overheating because the Vietnam War was raging and domestic social programs were putting inflationary pressure on the dollar. We had a market cap of $1 billion, and our stock was selling at 40 times earnings. I didn't think that could last. No matter how shrewdly we ran our company, deep down I knew our industry was cyclical and it was virtually impossible for any homebuilder to thrive when the business climate turned seriously down.

Conventional wisdom was—and is—that the safest diversification is into an industry closely related to your own. For Kaufman and Broad the safe plays would have been a lumber or furniture company. But I wanted something that would see us through the worst imaginable downturn, so I set our team to researching what sort of companies survived the Great Depression. Banks, of course, didn't do well at all. Depositors drained them of liquidity and, at the time, no federal protections existed to keep them afloat. Mortgage companies, left with huge unpaid home loans when borrowers couldn't afford payments, tanked.

The companies that seemed to do the best were life insurers. We discovered that even in bad times, everyone who can afford to holds on to their life insurance to provide security for their family, meaning insurance companies kept getting business through the Depression. Those who couldn't afford their premiums simply let their policies lapse. That meant the insurance company got to hold on to all the earlier payments but had no obligation to pay out on any future liability. Insurance companies could rest on their cash holdings, even if premiums declined and they had fewer customers on their books.

After we figured out that insurers survived the Depression relatively well, we started another exhaustive study: Which was the best insurance company to buy? I wanted one we could afford but with a long and solid reputation. The stable, family-run Sun Life Insurance Company of America fit the bill.

In 1974, Kaufman and Broad suffered its worst year to date and posted its first loss. The decade would only get worse for the economy, with a crushing energy crisis, inflation, and high unemployment that made buying a home impossible for many families. The malaise of the 1970s was quite different from the low of the 1930s. It was caused by an entirely new and, at the time, poorly understood set of circumstances that came to be called stagflation. But the key lesson of the 1930s, that insurers could ride out a severe downturn, still applied. By studying the past, I learned how to give our company, its employees, and its stockholders a better future.

No matter how much our economy evolves, some things never change. If you know history, you know the indicators of a downturn, whether it's the 1970s or 2009: job creation slows, consumer confidence dips, businesses don't know how to move toward growth, banks are cautious about lending, and the global financial markets tumble. That's when you know it's time to play defense.

Is *Core Competency* Just Another Term for Complacency?

The kind of CEO who heeds conventional wisdom and thinks with the herd never would have bought Sun Life. Life insurance was about as different from homebuilding as an industry could be. Wouldn't this new endeavor just become a dangerous distraction that we might mismanage while neglecting our primary business? I seriously considered the question, but if I had reasoned according to conventional logic, I never would have strayed from my "core competency" in accounting and still would be back in Detroit doing other people's taxes. Sometimes you can mistake what you're comfortable with for what you're good at. Unreasonable thinking is your ticket out of that trap.

As I came to realize, our company's core competency wasn't in building homes. It was in serving customers, particularly baby boomers. It was in meeting consumer needs at a price point that was advantageous to the buyer and profitable to us. We could do this in any industry. All we had to do was learn our new business from the inside out first—and there was no shortcut to that.

ONCE YOU'VE DONE YOUR HOMEWORK, PUT IN THE LONG EFFORT—IT WILL PAY OFF IN UNEXPECTED WAYS

When we bought Sun Life, we started to revamp it. We had no idea at the time that we were going to turn an insurance company into a retirement savings titan, or that we were transforming an old brand into a new and much improved one, or that we were building toward a big merger. We just wanted to run a better insurance company, and all we knew was that Sun Life didn't run very efficiently.

Most corporate acquisitions fail because companies are as different as people, with their own personalities and cultures. Bringing two firms under one roof rarely goes smoothly. We knew we needed to put in a lot of effort to ensure a successful integration.

I visited Sun Life's offices in Baltimore every month. I met with heads of departments, watched them work, and assigned some of my executives to figure out how best to improve the business. And we did improve it, steadily every year. We were one of the earliest users of optical imaging technology, which allowed us to turn paper files into electronic ones. (This was another instance of daily research paying off—I first read about optical imaging in a newspaper.) We applied computer software that enabled our agents to hand customers their policies immediately, rather than waiting the customary week or 10 days. After the acquisition of an Atlanta-based life insurer, we moved Sun Life to Atlanta, Georgia, to take advantage of that city's dynamism. It also pared down our workforce because many employees declined to make the move. Then we moved to Los Angeles, which allowed us to consolidate operations, keep close tabs on the business, and change the company culture from one with hundreds of low-paid clerks to one employing a few high-skilled professionals who were adept at using technology. We also managed to avoid layoffs because, frankly, most of the staff didn't want to move again.

Big Ideas Don't Happen in a Moment

It took us years of research on the insurance industry to find the niche where we could flourish—selling retirement products to aging baby boomers. After all that homework, a lot of effort, and the willingness to take a big risk, we had a smart and enormously profitable new business model.

That innovative strategy involved identifying our customers, figuring out what they wanted, and delivering it to them before and better than anyone else. In 1990 SunAmerica began its nearly decade-long run as the best performing stock on the New York Stock Exchange. In 1998 we merged the company with AIG for $18 billion. An investment of $10,000 in Kaufman and Broad when it went public in 1961, including the shares of SunAmerica received in the spin-off, would have been worth $34.1 million at the time of AIG's purchase. In other words, over that 37-year period, we outperformed even Warren Buffett's fabled Berkshire Hathaway.

But selling the company never was our goal. That seems to be the holy grail of many of today's entrepreneurs, fueled by stories of sudden wealth for very young innovators who cash out on a good idea. It may be a fine way to make money, and is the logical step for a business that needs capital or a parent company to expand to the next level. But founders, and anyone involved in a new business, still should act as if they're building a profitable, stand-alone company. Some great companies offer unquantifiable benefits to their customers—companies that would not have existed with less resilient founders. Mark Zuckerberg avoided the siren song of Yahoo! to keep Facebook independent.

Twitter's Evan Williams, in turn, refused to be acquired by Facebook and Google.

Focusing on a big sale isn't what creates success. If we had wanted to sell Sun Life, we could have, much earlier and for far less. But our only goal was to build a great business. In the end, it sold at a great price—for me, our shareholders, and our employees.

You Can't Do It All Yourself, So Ask Questions and Delegate

Sometimes you have to do your research on the run and learn while you're doing.

When my friend Alan Cranston asked me to chair his campaign for the U.S. Senate in 1968, I knew I had a lot to learn. Although I'm a lifelong Democrat, up until then, I had paid little attention to politics. My father was pretty liberal—he even supported the third-party progressive candidate against Harry Truman and Tom Dewey in 1948. I always had voted, but that was the extent of my participation. When I told Alan I knew nothing about campaigns, he just said, "You're smart. You'll figure it out." I was pretty busy running my company in what was a big year for us. We were expanding abroad and were gearing up to be the first homebuilder to be listed on the New York Stock Exchange. I could easily have told Alan that I just didn't have the time, or I could have tried to take a shortcut by not doing any research, settling into the role of a figurehead, as many chairs do. But that would have only hurt my friend's campaign.

Instead I accepted and then read everything I could about campaigning. I became the guy with the info so that Alan could focus on making speeches and shaking hands. I was always ready whenever he asked me questions about voters, donors, issues, and our rival candidate's platform. His questions, in turn, helped me sharpen my knowledge and skills.

Politics was a new world for me, and I did make some mistakes. I was blunter than I should have been in the media—speaking some harsh truths about our rival candidate, who I thought was a blowhard. I never minced words in business, but I probably should have been a little more artfully unreasonable in politics. Still, I was glad I took the job. At the end of that tumultuous year, Alan won the election and I had learned how to campaign for a cause and how to raise money—two skills that would come in very handy later on.

Like Alan, I make it a habit to ask everyone around me a lot of questions so I always know what's going on. Some people find this very unreasonable. They're used to the boss walking into a meeting and saying, "What's this all about?" Some CEOs think they can get away with that because they're at the top. Perhaps being underprepared is their way of showing how important they are. In fact, the boss should be the best informed person in the room and should have the good sense to ask questions when necessary. Even in the thick of things it's important to keep asking questions—and you won't be able to ask the right ones if you haven't done your homework. That's how you turn experience, yours or others', into an education.

Chapter 5

THE VALUE OF BEING SECOND

Before you can be number one, sometimes you have to be number two.

For a while during the 1990s, it felt like you had to be first to get anywhere. The beginning of the Internet age seemed to reward innovation above all else. Men and women who could create totally new technologies to serve markets that no one else thought existed became wealthy and successful virtually overnight.

But what you might call the first mover advantage always has been overrated and never more so than in the early years of the new digital economy. Consider the onetime kings of the 1990s and early 2000s: Netscape, Napster, WebCrawler, and Friendster. Netscape's browser had consumer goodwill and great market share, but Microsoft's Internet Explorer beat it by matching its features and being bundled free into new personal computers. Napster sunk under the weight of lawsuits, losing customers to its rivals, legal and illegal. WebCrawler could claim to be the first widely used search engine, but it couldn't keep up with the likes of Lycos or Infoseek. Friendster's social network couldn't match Myspace for customization and music integration. Then, a lot of these second movers were beaten out by still later comers like Google and Facebook. Who knows what may come along next?

FOLLOW THE SMART FIRST MOVERS

My first move in business was a second move: building houses without basements. Other homebuilders elsewhere had done it before Kaufman and Broad, and that gave us several advantages. We didn't need to conduct consumer research to know that people would buy these houses. That made it easier to ignore the condescension of older Detroit builders: "Young man, I've been in this business for 20 years and you just don't understand the market like I do." Sure, their disapproval gave me a little pause, but I knew we weren't attempting something completely untried.

Kaufman and Broad was the second mover again when we expanded to France in 1967. Levitt and Sons, the famed builder of the East Coast's "Levittowns," had set up shop in Paris three years before. Bill Levitt was the first to recognize that Europe would take longer to recover from World War II but that when it did, the housing market would boom as America's had right after the war.

Levitt was right about Europe, and I was smart enough to know it. Following him to France was something like following the first hiker on a trail. The guy in front has to break through the brush, get scratched up, and lose his way a few times before making it to the top. The second guy can just charge along the path the first guy has marked, avoiding the rough patches where he stumbled.

In Paris, our company went head-to-head with Levitt's and made a solid mark. Eventually, after some troubles with his corporate parent, Levitt had to shut down European operations, leaving us the only game in town. We went on to become Paris's biggest single-family homebuilder.

MARKETS EVOLVE AND FIRST MOVERS SOMETIMES CAN'T, OR WON'T, KEEP UP

Being the second mover isn't just a matter of timing. The first mover does have some advantages that may be hard to match: technological know-how, access to resources and talent, early market dominance, and name recognition. Each of these, however, can be acquired by a smart second mover. Technological know-how can be learned or surpassed. Even the company considered the final word in microchips, Intel, has ceded some market share to an up-and-coming rival, Advanced Micro Devices. Talent may go to the first mover, but that same talent won't be happy suppressing their entrepreneurial instincts just to stay employed at a steady first mover. Think of all the Facebook and Google employees who have gone on to start their own companies or join another start-up. A few of my Kaufman and Broad employees went on to become independent homebuilders.

Market dominance and name recognition can be harder to overcome. Sometimes a first mover defines an entire market so well that its name becomes synonymous with the product—such as Tupperware, Coca-Cola, Post-its, or TiVo. Fortunately for the rest of us, such companies are the exception, not the rule, and nothing lasts forever—not even for them. Xerox is a shadow of what it once was. Kodak, which used to be another way of saying snapshot, is now bankrupt. Polaroid suffered the same fate.

As you can see from these examples, a second mover can beat the first mover on branding and market share by relying on an unalterable commercial fact: markets evolve. Tastes and expectations don't stay the same. Niches grow more numerous, deeper, and, thanks to the Internet, more accessible. A first mover can sometimes fall in love with its product and fail to realize when technology evolves and consumers want something different. This leaves the field wide open for somebody new. The Big Three automakers were all second movers, improving manufacturing methods and offering a better product. General Electric wouldn't have become one of this country's largest companies if it had stuck to only manufacturing light bulbs. And Apple, the world's most valuable tech firm, has been a second mover several times. The company was not the first to sell mp3 players, smartphones, or even personal computers. Apple just did it better than anybody else.

First Movers Always Leave Some Room—You Just Need to Find It

As I learned with our homes without basements, a low price helps a second mover. Unburdened by the costs of research and testing, the second mover can cut prices, which will always be the best way to enter a marketplace dominated by a first mover. Buyers snapped up our first homes at Kaufman and Broad because they cost less than our competitors'.

Holding down your costs requires planning and discipline, but it lets you increase your margins while giving your customers a better price. In France, Kaufman and Broad was able to make more money on our homes than Levitt despite selling at a lower price. We did this, as we had done in America, by negotiating better contracts with suppliers and labor and by working far faster than our competitors did.

Low prices and attention to your own costs won't matter much, however, if you can't make the sale. Finding customers who aren't being served by the first mover allows second movers to get a foothold in the market. Look for needs your competitors don't satisfy. Look for disgruntled customers who deal with your competitor not out of loyalty but because there's no other option. Make yourself an attractive alternative.

Think of Home Depot, which had long been the giant of everything-under-one-roof hardware. Then Lowe's came along and managed to grab some market share by offering a distinct experience to their customers: smaller scale, better-organized stores, and friendlier customer service.

At SunAmerica we worked hard to offer the best customer service—one of our many ways of finding our niche among big financial services companies and the old-line insurers. Starting in 1983, we did all we could to make it easy for consumers to find SunAmerica through their financial planners, to buy great policies or innovative retirement products, and to get in touch with our customer service representatives. That meant having the best distribution network, the best technology, and, of course, the best products.

We started with distribution. We wanted the biggest sales force this side of Merrill Lynch's—the top retailer of financial services—and we got very close. We accomplished that ambitious expansion by buying up brokerages, so we had thousands of independent brokers across the country. That meant SunAmerica's customers had easy access to brokers in their own neighborhoods, who could guide them through investment decisions and explain our new products.

Beginning in 1990, after moving operations to Los Angeles and streamlining our back office to make it nearly paperless, we installed 24-hour toll-free information lines, a telephone line for the hearing impaired, and software that let our brokers more clearly demonstrate how our products worked. By 1995 our website was up and running, and soon after, customers could log in to look at their policy online— well before many of our rivals even had a Web address.

All of this made buying a SunAmerica policy a friendlier, more modern experience than buying from our competitors, enhancing our customers' sense of security in what was a major financial decision.

STUDY A FIRST MOVER'S FAILURE FOR CLUES TO SUCCESS

One of the biggest second moves of my career was taking over the fund-raising for the construction of the Walt Disney Concert Hall, a new home for the Los Angeles Philharmonic. It turned out to be a forceful reminder that in every aspect of life you can build on the experience of others, add your own innovations, and achieve success.

The effort to construct Disney Hall began in 1987, with a very generous $50 million donation from Lillian Disney, Walt's widow. A committee was formed to oversee additional fund-raising, design, and building. Architect Frank Gehry designed a strikingly beautiful building. But nine years later, when I stepped in, construction hadn't even started. The fund-raising committee had wasted a lot of time raising only a couple of million dollars from donors other than the Disney family, even though the project's cost looked like it would top $200 million.

If you're the second mover and the first mover has failed—whether you're starting a company, taking over a project, or pursuing a social or civic reform—you're in something of a dangerous position. People tend to think one failure follows another, or that it's contagious. They might assume that the first mover struck out because there was no way to succeed. That's what many people whispered about Disney Hall—that L.A. didn't care enough about its symphony, that none of the city's rich were willing to open their wallets for the project.

I didn't believe that. Failure is never preordained. Along with my friend Dick Riordan, then L.A.'s mayor, and our fellow fund-raiser, Andrea Van de Kamp, wife of the former California attorney general and head of the Music Center board, we found a smarter way to sell Disney Hall. We saw clearly that sniffing around all the philharmonic's old sources of funding just wasn't working.

Instead, we proclaimed that Disney Hall, when built, would be "the heart of the city," a defining landmark like the Eiffel Tower in Paris, Big Ben in London, the Statue of Liberty in New York, and the opera house in Sydney. I also argued that it would reinvigorate L.A.'s center, a place whose world-class potential was going almost wholly unrealized. Suddenly, Disney Hall was no longer about a symphony orchestra, the arts, or even philanthropic generosity. It was about Los Angeles's right to call itself a world-class city. We raised that $200 million and then some, and Disney Hall has become exactly what we promised.

Often, when a problem seems insoluble, it's because somebody needs to come along and reframe it. The second mover has the best perspective to do it.

WHETHER YOU'RE THE FIRST MOVER, THE SECOND, OR
THE LAST—JUST KEEP MOVING

This chapter may have given you the impression that it's too risky to be the first mover. Actually, it doesn't matter whether you move first or last as long as you keep innovating.

Innovation is especially important in today's most dynamic economic sectors. Barriers to entry are low. Initial costs might be nothing more than registering a domain name and getting a decent server. It took decades for Johnson & Johnson to gain its nationwide prominence in the consumer goods market. It took Google only a few years to completely marginalize every other search engine. The point is to keep moving, especially now, when everything moves faster.

At SunAmerica, for example, we updated our signature annuity product, the Polaris fund, almost every year subsequent to its introduction. When we launched the fund, we were first movers: The fund was the first to offer middle-class customers the ability to switch their money from fixed to variable annuities and back again without paying a fee each time. That meant when interest rates were high and the market was down, a customer could easily switch over to fixed annuities, which yield a higher return in that climate. If the opposite happened, the customer could move to variable annuities. The fund was also managed by a group of talented investment professionals—something no other annuity company offered at the time. We had to play a careful game of timing to keep ahead of second movers. We didn't want to cannibalize our own products, but we also didn't want to wait for our competitors to beat us.

Not everyone can be an original thinker, but everyone can be a rational one. Innovation doesn't always mean creating something from thin air that needs a patent or a copyright. It just means always looking for ways to improve, sharpen, and evolve what you do—whether it's refining a product, keeping up with new technologies in your line of work, or reaching new customers in new ways, all based on the lessons of the first mover. As I often say, let someone else go first and get the arrows in their back.

Chapter 6

HOW TO WORK 24/7 AND STILL GET 8 HOURS OF SLEEP

Peeople who have been in meetings with me have probably heard me say, "Let's move on." That's how I tell people they're on the verge of wasting my time. If they're lucky, they've never heard me say, "Anything else?" That means they've already wasted my time, and I'm not happy about it.

Time is the most valuable thing you have—and I'm not just talking about the minutes for which you're paid.

A lot of people want to take your time from you. They want to bend your ear about something that you've already talked over. They're dreading starting some task and they want you to become their accomplice in procrastination. You've probably done this yourself.

But every moment of your time matters. I try to be in control of all of my time—from the first hours after I wake, to the slower hours before bed, to all those little minutes that get eaten up by idle chatter during meetings. Being stingy with your time is the key to working 24/7 but still getting 8 hours of sleep, as I do almost every night.

WORK DOESN'T HAVE TO BE YOUR LIFE, BUT YOUR LIFE IS YOUR WORK

As my wife, Edye, often says, I am not great at the so-called work-life balance. I work all the time. I've even pursued my hobbies with the same intensity I apply to my work, from stamp collecting as a kid to art collecting as an adult. I never play golf because it takes too long, and the business connections it produces can be made just as easily over an early breakfast. I never stay anywhere—parties, museums, meetings—longer than 3 hours. That's my personal limit. In my view, there aren't many things that need to last more than 3 hours.

The work-life balance seems to be a favorite topic of life coaches, therapists, and self-help books. They believe it counteracts "workaholism," the damaging addiction to work. Some managers argue it's increasingly important to keep in mind as technology allows work to seep into all of our hours, wherever we are.

I'm not suggesting we should bark like Pavlov's dogs every time our BlackBerrys buzz, or sacrifice a weekend hike for a conference call that could have waited until Monday. And I do understand that as companies cut jobs in tough times, the employees who remain sometimes have to pull more weight than they can carry. That's when it's particularly important to enforce the 8 hours of sleep rule and to get peaceful time away from the office.

But I also know I'm happiest when my work and my life feel like one and the same, not like two opposites to be balanced. I am a workaholic because I consider everything I do part of my work. It's one reason I put our family name on buildings. I'm proud of what I do in the office and outside it.

I want even my leisure to be productive. It has to make me feel happier, healthier, and smarter. Since my days at Michigan State University, I've loved watching football. But I refuse to spend 3 hours watching a 1-hour game. So I TiVo all of the games I want to watch and then speed through the idle commentary, commercials, and half-time show and just watch the plays.

Know What You Have to Do, Which Is Less Than You Think

The best way to take control of your time is to know what you *must* do. Sometimes it can seem like we have to do absolutely everything. We have to exercise an hour a day, seven days a week. We have to reply immediately to every e-mail and phone call.

Thinking that everything is important, that every request from other people has to be answered with a yes, will make 24 hours seem inadequate. In fact, there are very few things that you truly have to do. This category should include only the things that make you run—the things you couldn't live or work without. Nothing else comes close to being crucial.

When I launched Kaufman and Broad, I knew there were two things I absolutely had to do. One was to get 8 hours of sleep. Without that, my other 16 hours just wouldn't be what they could be. The second was to make all the decisions about land, particularly when we began to treat it as a raw material.

Picking land to buy is the biggest decision a homebuilder makes. It can't be undone. If you choose incorrectly, it's a surefire way to lose money. But if you choose wisely, it's the quickest way to gain.

Where to buy land was not a decision I could afford to screw up. I never let anyone else have the final word on land as long as I was in charge of the company. From the time we were a local builder buying a few dozen lots to our years as an international company building thousands of houses a year, I signed off on every land decision. I made sure always to know where we were buying, what the market was like there, and what each lot would do for us.

Anyone in any job can narrow his or her task list to the one that really matters. That's the job that should get your greatest—in fact, undivided—attention. It's the decision you want to make at your most alert moments. It's the task that earns you your salary, pays for your free time, determines the success of your company, and—when you do it right—makes you feel the most capable and proud.

Not Everyone Needs 8 Hours

For some people, sleep seems incidental. If you're one of them, I envy you. Bill Clinton, who I have known since he was governor of

Arkansas, sticks out in my mind as someone who does exceptionally well with very little rest.

While he was president, he invited me to stay at the White House. It had been a long day and I was tired, so I went to bed a bit early. At 11:30 PM, I woke up to a knock on the door. The president's usher poked his head in and informed me that the president was in the solarium and wanted to chat. There wasn't much I could say except, "Sure."

President Clinton came in, sat down, and began talking about everything—the Russian election, the Taiwan Strait, Israel, and why Kentucky was the best of the Final Four in that spring's college basketball playoffs. We ended up going to bed not long before dawn.

Only a few hours later, we were up again for a meeting. He asked me how I had slept.

"Quickly," I replied.

Setting Priorities Means Being Disciplined, but Not Rigid

Without adequate rest, it's hard to take a disciplined approach to using your time or to setting priorities, which is what makes effective use of your time possible. Making land decisions was not, of course, the only thing required of me as CEO of Kaufman and Broad. I couldn't, say, slack off on reviewing our financials, ditch the shareholder call, or ignore meetings with analysts. For everything else I had to do, I prioritized.

Prioritizing isn't just about making a list and checking off the boxes. It is something you should be doing constantly. Circumstances change throughout the day—emergency meetings are called, colleagues dream up new initiatives, a sudden inspiration comes to you at the coffeemaker—and your priorities can't stay rigid. Be flexible but also keep in mind what's most important.

Being unreasonable will help you set your priorities. Keep them constantly in mind. Doing that will make a stray chat with a colleague who habitually interrupts you seem a lot less necessary, no matter how much you convince yourself that you're just being a team player or trying not to hurt anyone's feelings.

If at the end of the day your priorities aren't completed, start early the next day or take work home. If I want to go over costs with a fine-tooth comb, as I've done since the early days of my business career, I can do it after hours. I've very often held meetings at 7 in the morning or 7 at night. Some people have legitimate reasons to excuse themselves—a family dinner, a previous commitment—but most people balk just because they'd rather be on their couch. No matter all the ways technology makes it easier and less of a chore to do, people still seem too reluctant to let work in to their 5-to-9. If you're serious about getting ahead, you can't keep those hours completely free of work—and, if you find you always want to, maybe you're in the wrong business.

If You Can't Delegate, It's Not Them, It's You

Once you've identified your crucial tasks and sorted out your priorities, try to find a way to delegate everything else. The inability to delegate is one of the biggest problems I see with managers at all levels.

Maybe I was lucky that I started my career before technology arose to let us keep tabs on everything all the time. In the days before e-mail, I could have asked that my employees copy me on every piece of correspondence, but that would have taken a lot of time and paper.

But today, I know executives who want to be copied on everything their employees do and who check the price of their company's stock every 30 minutes. Such habits make it difficult to focus on your crucial tasks and your priorities. I never receive copies of e-mails unless it's essential. When I was at Kaufman and Broad and SunAmerica, I never checked the company's stock price except at close—if anything big happened during the day, I made sure someone was charged with telling me. And I never interrupt what I'm doing for the intrusion of some other task. If you're in a meeting with me, you have my full attention—and you'd better use it well.

The trick to delegating is to make sure your employees share your priorities. Bosses should make clear what qualifies as an emergency, which situations require a team, individual, or leader response, and how far each person's duties and abilities can be stretched.

Find the best people to whom you can delegate, and know their strengths and weaknesses. If you think you can do it better, delegate anyway and try as hard as you can to close that gap by giving your colleague or employee the right feedback. Then recognize and accept that just because someone does something a little differently than you would, that doesn't mean it's wrong. What counts is that your goals get accomplished at a sufficient level of quality.

The only thing you shouldn't delegate are your crucial tasks. The one time I did that at Kaufman and Broad, handing the reins to the wrong person, I paid for it dearly. I picked a very smart guy to take over as CEO for a few years while I focused on our insurance business. But he wasn't the strongest manager. He didn't keep as close an eye on land decisions, and some of his executives were roped into poor investments. They didn't control their costs—something I had insisted on with near-religious zeal when I headed the company.

If you're afraid to delegate, or if you delegate incorrectly, it's not your employees' fault—it's yours. It's up to you to recognize when an employee just isn't up to the task. In that case, cut your losses quickly.

TRY SAYING "LET'S MOVE ON"—EVEN TO ME

As much as I value my time, I value everyone else's too. A lot of executives act like their time is worth more than anyone else's. But I always respect an employee who guards his or her time, even from me. I start meetings punctually, and if I don't, I apologize. When I say, "Let's move on"—and you should try saying it a lot more—I'm protecting my time and yours.

The bottom line is, watch your time like you watch your money. And repeat after me: Let's move on.

Chapter 7

BRIGHT AND YOUNG IS A WINNING COMBINATION

Back in 1986, my then assistant, Bruce Karsh, gave me some bad news: he was leaving Kaufman and Broad.

Bruce was just 31 years old, but he had been my right-hand man for two years, and it hadn't been easy to recruit him. When I found Bruce, he was a rising lawyer at O'Melveny and Myers, Los Angeles's oldest and biggest law firm. He had also been a star student at Duke University and a clerk to now Supreme Court Justice Anthony Kennedy.

I had wanted Bruce to stay on with me at Sun Life for a long time. It had been a big year for us. We had just acquired the company that would get us going in the annuity business and would help make us a multibillion-dollar company. But Bruce left me for the same reason he first came—he was a bright guy with a lot of ambition. I said he could go on one condition: He had to find me an even more talented replacement. Bruce hemmed and hawed at first. He already had a candidate in mind but, he said, the senior partners at O'Melveny would kill him if he told me.

I was eager to have another O'Melveny alum. I had learned that bright young corporate lawyers often sit across the table from investment bankers and do the same work but for a lot less money and with less room to grow. It was a great talent pool in which to fish. Thankfully, Bruce finally gave me the name of Jay Wintrob.

Jay was 29 years old. He had graduated summa cum laude from the University of California, Berkeley, and gone to the Berkeley School of Law. Bruce gave Jay the nudge, and he applied for the assistant's position. Compared to Bruce, Jay was a little sedate. But he showed up on time for his interview at my house, asked good questions, knew Kaufman and Broad well, and showed that he was ready to leave a comfortable job for something more challenging at a company on the verge of major growth. I hired him on the spot. I always bet on youth over experience for experience's sake, and I was willing to do it again with Jay.

Sometimes You Are What You Wear

The technology sector famously relies on fresh ideas from young people. It has built a system of handing out venture capital for their innovations. When you walk into a meeting of entrepreneurs and venture capitalists, you can tell who's who pretty easily. The ones with the ideas are wearing sweatshirts. The ones with the money are in the suits, like me.

Actually, I've spent much of my career in industries where youth is not particularly valued—accounting, homebuilding, and insurance. I've been the youngest guy on construction sites and in boardrooms more times than I can count. I got my fair share of "Where's your father?" when I launched Kaufman and Broad. I started wearing a suit to work every day because I wanted to look older. Weighing 130 pounds and sporting a big grin most of the time didn't exactly encourage people to take me seriously. In those days, most home-builders were family operations run by older men who had inherited the business. They liked doing the same old thing in the same old place because that's what their fathers had done. Many of my competitors placed too high a premium on experience—that's part of why Kaufman and Broad and, later, SunAmerica were able to become such successful companies. We captured bright young talent, listened to new ideas, and—when they made sense—ran with them.

Until 1961, when Kaufman and Broad had just been listed on the American Stock Exchange, I had hired only a few employees, all trustworthy people, many of whom I knew before they came on board. I hired my first boss, Leroy Golman, away from his own accounting firm. I partnered with a couple of homebuilders I met in Detroit to launch in our second market, Phoenix, Arizona, in 1960. And I left another executive I recruited from a rival homebuilder in charge of our Detroit business when I moved my family to Arizona so that I could oversee our Sunbelt operations. When we went public, we suddenly had a lot of capital to become what we wanted to be—a national homebuilder. To do that, we needed fresh talent, and to find it, I went straight to Harvard Business School.

Interviews Don't Have to Be Tricky

At the time Harvard Business School was the top-ranked place to get a business education. I flipped through stacks of résumés, looking for sound educational backgrounds and other notable qualifications.

When I first started recruiting for our company, I conducted interviews myself in Cambridge, Massachusetts, flying in and attempting to woo starry-eyed grads away from New York investment banks and toward a West Coast homebuilder they hadn't heard of. Over time I developed a set of expectations for a good interview. I've never proposed the sort of riddles that would-be Microsoft or Google employees now have to suffer through. Although I'm sure it helps those companies reduce their sizable applicant pools, I believe there are less tricky ways to learn how well a candidate handles stress and how quickly and clearly his or her mind works out a problem.

I put the most emphasis, instead, on what an interviewee can show me. I want to see a lot of confidence, ambition, and drive. I want him or her to ask me a lot of questions and to convey knowledge about the industry and my company. Even in the days before Internet search engines, I expected anyone applying for a job with me to get to the library and read some trade publications and company filings. With today's easy online searches, there's simply no excuse for not doing your homework.

Sometimes I missed hiring the best man or woman. On one of my trips to Harvard Business School, I interviewed a young man named Gary Wendt and decided not to bring him on board. Decades later I ran into him again. I was considering pursuing a merger for SunAmerica with General Electric, and Gary was CEO of General Electric Capital Services. He reminded me that I had once shown him the door. "Biggest mistake of my life," I told him. Gary was a good sport and put in a word for SunAmerica with GE's CEO Jack Welch, who, unfortunately, had by then soured on big financial services acquisitions. Jack probably wouldn't have paid the premium I believed SunAmerica deserved anyway.

QUALIFICATIONS ARE ALMOST EVERYTHING

Particularly for younger employees, the résumé doesn't always tell the whole story. That was certainly the case for Jana Greer, who came to me wanting to join Kaufman and Broad's communications department.

Jana had a solid educational background. She had studied speech communications and graduated Phi Beta Kappa. What she lacked was a compelling employment history. The only job she had held since graduation was as a guest relations manager at Disneyland. That didn't faze me. She gave an impressive interview, and I hired her. I had a feeling she had the potential to go on to great things.

I knew I had made the right decision when, years later, I was in Montreal on my way to France and I received her panicked phone call. Jana—the former communications student and now corporate communications vice president—was on a press check for our annual report and had spotted a major accounting error in our set-to-print financials. She had fact-checked the work of Price Waterhouse. She had grown a lot from when she was hired, as many young employees do. Their talent and energy spills into every part of a company. Jana moved from our homebuilding business to SunAmerica. She would go on to run our annuities division and ably shepherd the company through the financial troubles of its current parent and the 2008 economic crisis. Today, she is president and CEO of SunAmerica Retirement Markets.

How to Keep 'Em Once You Hire 'Em

Hiring the best young employees is a lot easier than keeping them. When I first started recruiting for Kaufman and Broad, I was up against the biggest names in American business: Goldman Sachs, General Electric, McKinsey & Company, Merrill Lynch, J.P. Morgan. I had to convince top-flight B-school graduates why they should work with me and not join a bigger company that might offer larger salaries.

The first thing I promised was stock options. Many young Kaufman and Broad employees became millionaires because of them. Commonplace today, that form of compensation was far rarer decades ago. The plus side of stock options remains the same: They give employees a reason to stick around and help the company grow. Tying an employee's compensation to the company's performance is a powerful incentive for everyone to work together toward the same goal. Employee stock ownership works at all levels of a company hierarchy, not just for top executives. We widened our plan to include more managers and gave almost all employees the ability to purchase our stock at a discount—at the suggestion of a 26-year-old employee.

The second promise I make young employees is even more important: I promise them growth. I recruited Bruce Karsh and Jay Wintrob away from a top-drawer law firm with a very simple question:

"Do you want to walk through the same door for the rest of your life, or do you want to do more?" It's exactly what an ambitious young person wants to hear. The only people who won't be swayed by that challenge are people you don't really want to hire. As Jay later told me, he switched because he wasn't sure what other opportunities he would have to try something outside his comfort zone at a law firm.

Our company delivered for both Bruce and Jay. We had a meritocracy through which they could rise quickly. Within eight years of leaving Kaufman and Broad, Bruce had cofounded an investment management firm, Oaktree Capital Management, that would make him a billionaire. As for Jay, within eight months, he was elected a corporate vice president of SunAmerica. In a few years he was executive vice president. In roughly the amount of time it would have taken him to become a partner at O'Melveny, he was managing SunAmerica's $25 billion investment portfolio.

Jay's path shows the third and most important thing I give young employees: I promise them hard work and high expectations all the time. Some employers think the young are allergic to hard work or that they'll slavishly put in 16-hour days because they don't have families yet. Neither is quite correct. Younger employees simply have fewer preconceived ideas of what they can and can't do. I always try to widen their perspective, deepen their sense of accomplishment, and build their capacity.

As Jay noticed quickly, I was not about to spend time asking him, or anyone, about the weekend or the outcome of Monday Night Football. But I did give him difficult work that he accomplished even when he thought he couldn't. His projects spanned every part of the company. He had no predestined career path. He worked on acquisitions, structured new business, disposed of old businesses, invested in private equity firms and hedge funds, and even advised me on hiring new employees—it sure worked when Bruce did it. Most important, he was my second-in-command when I negotiated SunAmerica's $18 billion merger with AIG.

After Jay had spent 13 years with the company—and only after I had searched exhaustively for the best candidate, inside and outside our company—I named him CEO of SunAmerica.

Youth Can Be a Risky Bet

Many employers might have seen Jay as a risk. He had a legal background, not a business one, and had never indicated he wanted to pursue a career in finance. I couldn't have known whether he would one day return to a law firm, start his own practice, or, for all I knew, write the great American novel. Jay stayed, I believe, because of the opportunities SunAmerica offered and because he enjoyed meeting the relentless expectations I had of him. Challenge and reward build loyalty.

Another top executive at my company, Bruce Karatz, started out as a risk too. He was untested when I hired him in Los Angeles and later put him in charge of building houses in the south of France. We had expanded to Europe only a few years earlier, but we had quickly made a name for our company against the other dominant American homebuilder operating there, Levitt and Sons. Soon after, the top position in our Paris operation opened when the manager and I disagreed over how much time he should spend on business versus polo ponies, parties, and mistresses, which I've seen can be a problem for executives at any age.

I was in Paris with Bruce searching for new candidates when, over lunch, he applied for the job. Oh great, I thought. This isn't going to go well. He was brand-new, but I knew he had ambition, big ideas, and a good work ethic. He reminded me of the men I had hired more than a decade earlier, when Kaufman and Broad was just getting off the ground—men I thought of as romantic dreamers but who still worked hard and definitely livened up the place. I didn't tell Bruce all that. Instead, at that Paris lunch, I goaded him with a little challenge, "You may fail, but go for it." Bruce thanked me and off he went.

In 1977, after a bruising few years for our business, he pulled off an incredible marketing feat. I was always looking for smart ways to sell our company's product, but I focused mostly on creating consumer value and on fairly straightforward, smart advertising. Bruce was keen on the newer way of the world, of much more attention-grabbing events and associations that created a personality for a company— what's now commonly called branding. I wasn't about to stifle that impulse, even though when Bruce told me what he wanted to do I thought he was nuts.

Bruce decided to build a model home on top of one of Paris's grand old department stores, Au Printemps. He had subcontractors pitch in labor and materials pretty much for free. He got the department store to furnish and landscape the models beautifully, and at no charge to us. He supervised workers as they hauled 1,000 concrete blocks, 7,000 roof tiles, 800 cubic meters of soil, several trees, and even a car up eight stories of Parisian splendor. Half a million people walked through the model home, including me. I was impressed. It was probably the most successful promotion in the history of home-building—until Bruce beat himself in 1997 by building an actual version of the cartoon house from *The Simpsons*. Our company became well regarded and a widely known name in France, and 11 years after Bruce proved himself in Paris, I named him chief executive of Kaufman and Broad.

OLDER PEOPLE CAN BE YOUNG TOO

I have been fortunate to have had four careers. Each one has kept me from getting too satisfied with myself. Each one has enabled me to keep learning, asking questions, thinking on my feet, and meeting bright people who are very different from me. Surrounding myself in my late 70s with talented young people keeps my viewpoint youthful. The problem with age isn't age—it's that every accomplishment can become an invitation to self-satisfaction and complacency. People often ask me how I've celebrated some of my achievements, from making my first million to breaking ground on The Broad, our contemporary art museum, in downtown Los Angeles in 2011. The answer is I don't. I move forward because I know I can do more.

The brightest young people instinctively know that the best is yet to come and that they have to work to get there. People of any age can cultivate those qualities, and it keeps them flexible and innovative. When I interview more experienced employees for a position, I always ask them: "What did you learn in the past year that you didn't know before?" Too often they have a hard time answering. That makes my decision an easy one.

Chapter 8

RISK

When you try something new or different, it may or may not work. That's how I define risk.

The earlier you start taking risks, the more comfortable you will become with them. When you're young, you don't have a lot to lose, and you have a lot of time to recover when things don't work out.

My first school of risk was the racetrack. You can't win if you don't bet, but you quickly learn not to wager more than you can afford to lose. There's an old saying among savvy horseplayers: never bet scared money.

I'm lucky that my wife, Edye, always understood and never shied away from risk. Like me, she's an optimist. When we went on our honeymoon in Florida, she didn't want to return home to snowy Detroit. I remember her saying, "Why don't we stay here? We're just starting out. We can start here."

She was not kidding. And she was right—we had very little to lose, so taking the risk of moving suddenly to a new place could have paid off big. Although we didn't move to Florida, her words rang in my head the next year, when I decided to start our homebuilding company.

To some extent, taking risks is a matter of temperament, the willingness to dare big. But everyone can train themselves to try it.

The first risk is exhilarating, not because it's big but because you have nowhere to go but up. Legendary entrepreneurs from Andrew Carnegie to Bill Gates all made one starting gamble and won a lifetime of reward.

From the moment you *take* your first risk—starting a business, embarking on a new career, or making a new investment—you'll start to learn how to *manage* risk. The good news is nothing will seem as scary as that initial leap.

CLINGING TO SAFETY IS MORE IRRATIONAL THAN TAKING RISK

I keep a copy of *Against the Gods: The Remarkable Story of Risk* by Peter L. Bernstein in my office. As the book shows, our concept of risk as something to be managed is old, but not ancient. It arose when humans realized the future is not just the whim of some divine force. Risk grew more predictable with the invention of probability theory, but it remained—and will always be—a gamble against larger forces, like economics, politics, technology, and sometimes what passes for common sense. Still, in the face of less-than-divine power, risk has become ever more manageable.

Whether you're naturally inclined toward risk or you're not, "managing risk" can sound quite unreasonable, or even like an oxymoron. If you love the thrill, you're not going to like the idea of managing it. And if you hate risk, you're not going to believe it can be managed. But taking carefully measured and balanced risks has allowed me to take big gambles without losing sleep.

At SunAmerica we incorporated risk management into the way we calculated our investment income. We managed risk by having a diversified portfolio and by limiting the amount of noninvestment-grade high-yield bonds. This method let us take on risky investments without becoming a risky company. We took as many different kinds of risks as we could—risks that weren't correlated, new asset classes, securities we originated. It's a popular way to build a portfolio now, although it was less tried then.

SunAmerica's portfolio may not have looked good in any given year compared to a more conservative—or a riskier—company. A portfolio made up of just treasury bonds might have performed better, or a high-risk portfolio of so-called junk bonds might have yielded higher returns. But our goal was not to beat everyone every year. Looking over three, four, or five years, it was clear that we had far better performance than both the most conservative companies and those that took on the most risk.

ASKING THE KEY QUESTIONS

Ask yourself two questions before you take on a risk: What do I have to lose? And what's the worst that can happen?

I always ask these questions, and I take them seriously. When I started Kaufman and Broad, the answers were my father-in-law's capital, and I could return to accounting (which would allow me to pay back my father-in-law). When I'm considering investing in a company or a fund, asking these questions reminds me that I can always sell. And if I have to sell my investment at a loss, I can make it up in the future.

By asking these questions, you'll often see the real potential cost of a risk you shouldn't take—like investing in a dubious type of security or buying a home you can't quite afford. But a lot of times you'll realize that you don't have much to lose, and the worst-case scenario is something you can overcome. Asking and answering these questions can help you transform yourself from an "Of course not" thinker into a "Why not?" thinker. Holding on to "Of course not" thinking can paralyze you in the face of risk.

RISK CAN BE CONTAGIOUS—DON'T CATCH THE DEADLY KIND

SunAmerica's habit of risk management meant our company was always interested in taking risk, but risk wasn't what motivated us. I've encountered many people who seem driven purely by risk—which almost always leads to a fall.

After the end of the recession in the early 1980s, Wall Street rose from the ashes and had a legendary decade. The years were immortalized in film and literature—from the "greed is good" motto of Gordon Gekko in Oliver Stone's *Wall Street* to the gripping nonfiction books with tellingly extreme titles, such as *Liar's Poker, Den of Thieves*, and *Barbarians at the Gates.*

Kaufman and Broad was riding high in the 1980s. We could have played it fast and loose like the characters in those books and movies. We had survived the 1970s, unlike many homebuilders. Baby boomers were starting to buy first or second or third houses. Our insurance company was going strong, with a new mission to serve the boomers and a growing investment portfolio. Investors and banks trusted us with their money.

NEVER BET THE FARM—OR EVEN HALF THE FARM

I managed to avoid junk bonds during the 1980s, unlike many other companies. Michael Milken's Drexel Burnham Lambert trading desk in Beverly Hills, California, was just a few miles from my office. To finance start-ups and leveraged buyouts, he sold a lot of securities with very low credit ratings on the promise of very high returns. Anyone looking closely at these assets knew they were dangerous. I kept all unusual investments to less than 10 percent of SunAmerica's portfolio—my personal rule of thumb because I knew we could afford to lose some of the 10 percent—although many people tried to convince me to go higher. Companies that made bigger bets, putting as much as half their assets in junk bonds, didn't make it through the decade.

The key for me was never to fall into the successful entrepreneur's most common trap: the illusion of invincibility. We're an optimistic bunch, but we can never lose sight of the downside. My inability to ignore it has kept me in business a long time. Maybe it's because I grew up in the Great Depression. Maybe it's because I manage to keep my head on straight no matter the noise of the business world around me. I always analyze the worst-case scenario and the consequences of failure.

There are some exceptions to my 10 percent rule. If you're young and have a lot of options, or if you have a great Plan B or some other project set to pay off, then you can raise your risk a little more. But I like to bet no more than 10 percent. That's how I've survived so many ups and downs.

Even Edye, so carefree on our honeymoon in Florida, put her foot down after my first risk, when I started a business despite having a big mortgage to pay. She made me promise that we would never have another mortgage. I'm happy to say I stuck by that promise, even though it's not the smartest financial move, as you'll learn in Chapter 10.

Chapter 9

HOW TO GET RESULTS

I have a reputation for being difficult to work with.

Whether it's raising money for a cultural institution or insisting on the maximum gallery space in a new museum, I prefer to think that I keep the ultimate goal in mind, and I'm impatient with anything that gets between where we are now and where we need to be. But you can't just roll over other people—that would be irrational. You have to try to persuade them. I've learned how to do it in an artfully unreasonable way, in business and in philanthropy.

It's a lot easier to persuade if you're talking to the right person. When I needed capital to start our homebuilding company, Edye suggested that I ask her father, Morris Lawson.

Morris was a self-made businessman. He had grown up poor, the only one of his parents' 10 children to make it to college, where he studied chemistry. From its sturdy brick headquarters in Detroit, his business—the Morris Extract Co.—sold extracts, bitters, liqueurs, syrups, and concentrates to hospitals, schools, cafeterias, and bars.

I knew Morris was a good person to approach because we had a strong relationship, he was an experienced entrepreneur, and, most important, he had the means and motive to help. He was a keen thinker and willing to extend himself to be part of a good idea. (Everyone should have such a father-in-law.)

Edye and I liked to have dinner with her parents once a week—not only because we were fond of them, but also because neither of us knew how to cook. I gave Morris my pitch at one of our weekly dinners. I wasn't nervous because I was convinced that my idea to start a homebuilding company would succeed. In laying out my vision, I demonstrated to Morris how much homework I had done and how well I knew the housing market. I told him why there was a demand for homes without basements, who our target customer base would be, and why it made sense to set a low price for our product. I had worked out all the numbers and sketched out what our balance sheet and our cash flow would look like—something anyone starting a new business should do. I explained that I had an experienced partner on board, Donald Kaufman, who Morris knew because Donald's wife was Edye's cousin.

Morris could quickly see that we had a good idea, some experience, and a lot of drive, not to mention that our success would lead to a comfortable future for his daughter. He sold some stock to give us the $12,500 we needed. It was an enormous sum at the time, and he gave it to me with no more collateral than a handshake. As it turned out, we shared not only a deep love for Edye but also a disdain for conventional wisdom.

Without that timely first investment, I probably would have had to stick to accounting for quite a while before I had enough money to start a business. In return, Don and I gave Morris some equity in the company—and that proved to be one of his most lucrative investments.

Make Sound Promises and Offer Something in Return

Many years later, when Edye and I had settled our family in Los Angeles and collecting contemporary art had become one of my private passions, I was asked to help establish the Museum of Contemporary Art (MOCA) and become its founding chairman. Los Angeles was one of the few major American cities at the time without a contemporary art museum, despite having great art schools and a significant population of talented working artists whose output was going into collections and museums all over the globe. The museum would be essential if Los Angeles hoped to become an internationally respected center of the arts and benefit from all the tourism, arts education, and other opportunities that would come with that status.

Getting MOCA off the ground was a major test of my ability to get things done, and it's where I learned my technique for getting results—to go to the other guy's turf, to have a stake in the deal, and to only make promises I can keep.

The opportunity to build MOCA grew out of a clever rethinking of city rules. Los Angeles required developers to take a small percentage of their overall costs and spend it on public art. Often that meant a bad piece of sculpture in a lobby—not exactly what public art should be. Fortunately, Los Angeles's visionary mayor, Tom Bradley, was willing to combine all the developers' fees from a massive project to rebuild Bunker Hill and put the sum toward a new museum—but only if we could raise a $10 million endowment through private donations. I joined forces with Judge William A. Norris, collector and arts advocate Marcia Weisman, and a few others to raise that money.

It was 1979, and although I was eager to see the new museum built, I had never been responsible for raising so much cash. I started by doing my homework, beginning with a visit to the grande dame of L.A.'s cultural philanthropy, Dorothy Chandler. I had met Mrs. Chandler, or Buffy, as a lot of people called her, only a couple of times at social events, but I knew she was a legendary fund-raiser for cultural projects like the Hollywood Bowl and the Music Center. I figured she could give me advice, and I thought it would be courteous to notify her of what we were doing.

I set up a meeting with her at her home—a stately old mansion in the Hancock Park neighborhood with towering columns that made it look like a branch of the Bank of England. Going forward with the MOCA campaign, I would always visit people at their homes or offices when I was asking them for help. It's a gesture of respect to go to them when you're asking for something, and you're likely to get a more sympathetic ear if your listener is in his or her comfort zone.

Buffy helpfully told me the basics of putting together a fundraising campaign but declined to help, which didn't surprise me. Members of her family and her circle of supporters were deeply committed to the Los Angeles County Museum of Art and, perhaps, they feared our new museum would compete with that institution's contemporary art program. In any event, it was clear we wouldn't have her participation.

Without Buffy on board, I thought it might be best to put my money where my mouth was. I couldn't convince anyone unless I clearly demonstrated my own commitment to the new museum, so I pledged the first $1 million, payable over five years, to an institution that did not and might never exist. I always like paying a pledge over time because I can keep the total sum invested and I've hedged my risk if the project collapses.

With L.A.'s old money beyond our reach, I knew we had to come up with a new approach. Fortunately, I had a great partner to work with—the MOCA campaign was where I first met Andrea Van de Kamp. We came up with an alternative to traditional capital campaigns. We reimagined the potential universe of givers and made provisions for a much larger donors' pool. Anyone who gave more than $10,000 would be called a founder of the museum, and his or her name would be prominently displayed in the museum's entrance. That was an easy promise to keep but a very enticing one that gave us access to more than the usual suspects from whom to raise our money. Within a couple of years, and boosted by a few seven-figure gifts from businesses like ARCO, our "founders" innovation raised $13 million from about 600 donors.

If you're flexible about creating opportunities to participate in a good idea, you may be surprised how many people are willing to help you. That's the thing about good ideas: People want to be part of them, so make sure that's what you're pitching.

PERFECT YOUR PITCH, AND MAKE IT BIG

Two decades later, I was asked to spearhead the fund-raising for a stalled civic project on Bunker Hill—Frank Gehry's Walt Disney Concert Hall. It would require all the persuasion an unreasonable man could muster.

I knew the project held the potential to create not only a much-needed new home for the city's world-class philharmonic orchestra but also a visual icon representing L.A.'s emergence as a global cultural capital. The problem was, despite the Disney family's generous gifts to build the hall, other donations would be required and the campaign to secure them was going nowhere. People had begun to whisper that Gehry had designed an unbuildable hall—at least at a cost anyone could afford. The County of Los Angeles, which had granted Disney Hall its lease and had pitched in for a parking lot below the venue, threatened to declare Disney Hall in default if $50 million couldn't be raised by July 1, 1997. But the *New York Times* and other media had covered the project, and architectural journals had lauded its design. We couldn't just abandon it. It was a question of civic pride.

I first studied the mistakes the campaign had made so far—a lack of controls, poor budgetary discipline, and an inability to pitch the hall in a persuasive way. I decided to convince our donors by focusing on how important the hall was to Los Angeles. They didn't have to care about the symphony or architecture—they just had to care about their city.

When it was time to pick my allies, I knew who to call. I enlisted my former MOCA colleague Andrea Van de Kamp again. She has a natural charm and an ability to get anyone on the phone. I also knew that a pitch based on the good of the city needed a particular kind of credibility, so I brought on Dick Riordan, then the city's mayor.

Right away, Dick and I knew we would have to demonstrate that we believed our own pitch. We both contributed money immediately to signal our commitment to and confidence in the project. We told donors that their money would only be used for construction and gave them a guarantee: They would get their money back if the hall wasn't built.

By the county's July 1 deadline, we raised nearly $100 million, or almost double what the county had required to save the project. We got off to a great start, and we would go on to raise more than $200 million total. Even a good idea looks better when people can see that you're tangibly committed to it—and getting your way is easier when people can see the direction you're headed.

Chapter 10

LEVERAGE

If you have ever bought anything on credit, you've used leverage.

Let's say you put some money you had saved down on a car and finance the rest. With the loan, you have to pay five years of interest—not an inconsiderable sum. But you get the car right away, and all the opportunity it brings: picking up your date, taking a road trip, and of course, driving to your job to make the money you need to pay off your car loan. The car may not be "worth" the money you paid plus interest—certainly not after you've driven it around for five years—but living without a car carries its own costs.

Without the loan, you would have whatever amount you had for a down payment, but you would have to spend at least a few years saving up the rest of the car's purchase price. And you would probably be taking the bus—making it that much harder to do everything you want to do, including making a living.

The loan is your leverage—it's what enables you to do more with your money.

But leverage isn't always money. Sometimes it's about channeling your energy and effort, enlisting the help of your friends and colleagues, applying technology, working with the press or social media, or mentoring someone who goes on to mentor 10 more people.

I've used leverage to increase capital for my businesses, but I've also used it to get the most out of my marketing, to raise funds for civic initiatives, and to do more in philanthropy than we possibly could have with our money alone.

Think of the literal meaning of the word *leverage*. It refers to levers—tools that amplify your power to move something. They're everywhere, and you should always use them when you can.

Some Straight Talk About the Mother of All Loans—Your Mortgage

Buying a home using a mortgage is the best opportunity most people have to leverage their money.

I recognize the reluctance to get a mortgage. When we bought our first house, Edye always said that she hated the idea of "mortgaging the nest." Despite not carrying mortgages myself, I still think they're one of the best forms of leverage when used correctly. In fact, they were essential to the spread and growth of American wealth in the twentieth century. The benefits that flow from being a nation of homeowners are incalculable.

Mortgages are dangerous only if you let them control you. If you agree to take on a mortgage you can't comfortably carry, then you're going to get into trouble. That's part of what inflated the housing bubble. When it popped, it triggered the financial crisis we are living through today. But a mortgage you can handle is a great way to use leverage.

As in the case of the hypothetical car, when you buy a house, you're getting a lot in return, even if the house will never be worth what you end up paying after 30 years of principal and interest. But you're buying a home where you can live with your family, developing a stake in a neighborhood and a community—and by not paying rent, you're building equity in an investment. You're earning good credit if you pay your mortgage on time. And you can purchase what you never could have afforded using only your own money. Plus you get tax deductions on your mortgage interest.

When interest rates are really low, you should pay as little down as possible. I know this sounds risky, especially considering the recent housing crash. But it works as long as you invest money that would have gone into a down payment in a solid mutual fund that appreciates at a higher rate than the mortgage interest you're paying. You're increasing the value of your dollar by using someone else's money.

SPREAD THE WEALTH—HOW TO LEVERAGE DOING GOOD

When you use a mortgage to buy a house, you're using your dollars to help create stability for you and your family. And because of your mortgage, you have more money left over to do whatever you want: pay for your children's piano lessons, start a business, or donate to a cause. Your mortgage increases the amount of good you can do for yourself, your family, your neighborhood, and the world.

Imagine the power of leveraged dollars devoted solely to doing good. Edye and I had a lot more dollars for just that purpose after we merged SunAmerica with AIG. We established The Eli and Edythe Broad Foundation to fund scientific research and education reform, the work of which I'll discuss in a later chapter. We combined it with The Broad Art Foundation, which we had started in 1984, to create The Broad Foundations.

The Broad Art Foundation is a prime example of leveraging wealth to do more. Edye and I ran out of wall space for our art and wanted to keep collecting. We also wanted the contemporary art we loved to be accessible to the public, so we decided to create a foundation that would serve as a lending library, a public collection from which museums could borrow works. Rather than keeping our collection to ourselves, we leveraged the pleasure and stimulation the artworks could bring by making them accessible to audiences around the world.

EXTEND THE POWER OF YOUR DOLLAR—FIND MONEY THAT COSTS LESS THAN YOURS

As our personal and foundation art collections grew to approach 2,000 works, Edye and I decided we wanted to have a permanent home for them. Estimates suggested building a museum would cost between $100 million and $150 million. That money would have to come from the same pot Edye and I use to fund all of our philanthropic efforts. The withdrawal of that much money would mean that the foundations' portfolio would earn significantly less, thus reducing the amount we had available to give to grantees. We had to find a way to use leverage to avoid an outright payment of tens of millions of dollars.

As we thought about the museum, Edye and I wanted to create an institution that would exist in perpetuity, long after we were gone, so we formed a new nonprofit to build and operate the museum. To ensure its independence and longevity, we appointed an autonomous governing board of professionals with strong financial, artistic, and organizational expertise.

The museum board recommended that we leverage The Broad Foundations's assets to pay for the construction and operation of the museum. The board asked us to award a multiyear grant to the museum so that it could use that pledge as collateral to borrow the money.

The museum board then decided to issue tax-exempt bonds, something a nonprofit can do at a low interest rate. That's how museums like the Getty, the Museum of Modern Art, and the Los Angeles County Museum of Art have raised money to construct new buildings or finance expansions.

The museum sold $150 million worth of Aa1-rated bonds, promising to pay them back in 10 years at 3.13 percent interest. Investment bankers told us it was crazy to expect that a brand-new entity with no credit history would get even an A1 rating. But we picked Morgan Stanley as our underwriter because they believed it could be done. They and our team of lawyers delivered what conventional wisdom said was unreasonable.

The bond's sale was a win for all parties. Our foundations preserved their endowment so that the earnings could continue funding work in education reform, scientific and medical research, and the arts. Bondholders will get their money back, plus interest. The museum received the money it needs to build. And the people of Los Angeles will get a new museum.

If possible, you should always try to make leverage work to save you money. If the interest on a loan is lower than what you earn on your investments, always take the loan. There are risks—if your investments falter, or if the loan comes with particular conditions—but if you've managed the risks properly and are confident of your investments' strength, you'll be in great shape.

LEVERAGING PEOPLE AND EFFORT WORKS JUST AS WELL AS LEVERAGING MONEY

Leveraging isn't just about money.

I learned that on my first major fund-raising campaign. When raising money for the Museum of Contemporary Art back in the early 1980s, I had far less money available to give to good causes. I put up $1 million—a lot for our family then—because that was as far as we could go. (If you're giving money and you want to do it right, make it hurt a little. That will keep you invested in what you're doing and make you watchful of the cause you're supporting.)

But I didn't stop my work there with a donation. I organized the overall fund-raising campaign, using my initial contribution as my leverage. I told everyone I knew who had the ability to donate that I had put up some money, so why shouldn't they? I never could have given $13 million outright, but that's the total we reached—$3 million more than the city required before they would release funds to build the museum.

More recently, Edye and I used our philanthropic dollars to leverage government spending. We saw a perfect opportunity when Californians approved a $3-billion ballot proposition in 2004 to fund stem cell research. At the time, federal regulations severely limited labs funded by federal dollars from pursuing embryonic stem cell research.

Because almost all California labs received some federal funding, Edye and I quickly realized that the state needed new facilities where stem cell research could be conducted without restriction. I had read about the issue and saw, as a layperson, the potential of stem cell research. We started with the University of Southern California (USC), where I sat on the board of the USC Keck Medical School, and gave them the funds to build a stem cell research center. Then we gave to UCLA, which had usable buildings but lacked operating funds and the necessary equipment. We also made a grant to UC San Francisco, where we were impressed with the work of young scientists and the quality of the researchers, to build a cutting-edge center. By the time we were through, we had given a carefully targeted $75 million to create badly needed institutions.

Although we had no grand plan at the time we made these donations, I do see biomedical research as essential to the economic future of California. Over time our investments will pay off not only in lives saved or made livable, but also in jobs and greater prosperity for our state.

If you're using leverage to do good, talk up what you're doing, whether it's making a donation or volunteering, and persuade others to join you. Leveraging dollars is important, but your time and energy are among the most valuable resources you have—why not make them go further?

I'm particularly proud of our use of leverage in education reform. That's where we've managed to leverage the work of hundreds of smart, driven professionals.

We recognize that a great teacher in every classroom is the most important factor in a student's success. But it would be virtually impossible for us to work with the millions of teachers in classrooms across America. By focusing our efforts on training school district superintendents—essentially the CEOs of school districts that are often larger than many Fortune 500 companies—we realized they had the power to put effective teachers in every classroom.

Our superintendents extended the reach of our money many times over. We couldn't afford to train 100,000 teachers. But we could train 100 superintendents, who could have an impact on more than 100,000 classrooms.

If you're a teacher, I admire you, and you already know the power of leverage. You devote your time and energy to educating children, who grow up to be innovative, productive, and philanthropic adults. Every hour you give, the world will get back many times over. The value of that effort is priceless.

Chapter 11

MARKETING

I've always been a salesman.

Like many ambitious boys of my generation, I started out peddling the *Saturday Evening Post* door to door. Later it was stamps and, in high school, women's shoes. I told all my customers they looked good, which sent them home happy—even if the shoes pinched.

During college I moved on to selling garbage disposals. Each morning, I would drive to an address chosen by my bosses, haul the disposal out of my trunk, and carry it from house to house in my rumpled suit and tie. I was usually drenched in sweat by the time some kind housewife invited me inside to demonstrate my product. I would recite a prepared speech about sanitation and the strength of our disposals and point out that a "dishmaster" came free with every purchase. (The dishmaster was a water-powered brush that connected to a sink's faucet with a flexible rubber tube. It was a popular accessory in those pre-dishwasher days.) While my pitch was in progress, I dropped glass marbles into the disposal, which crushed them. The marble gimmick always impressed customers because they didn't realize any disposal could effortlessly break a marble.

From that job I learned to project a lot of confidence. Nothing teaches perseverance like forcing yourself to knock on another door after one slams into your nose. Your confidence can make whatever you're trying to sell—whether it's a business plan to investors, an idea to your boss, or a product to a customer—sound irresistible.

I also learned that confidence may get you one sale, but overconfidence can lead you to forget to ask yourself: What do customers want and need? That's the key to marketing. It was the first thing we considered at Kaufman and Broad, and I continued to ask it throughout my business career. The answer we came up with—and this is always the answer—is value. No matter how much money your customers have, they still want value.

Know Your Customers and What Moves Them

At Kaufman and Broad, we focused on the first-time homebuyer. These customers were always simpler to work with. You never had to wait for them to sell their existing house. Their preferences were less complicated than those of wealthier families or buyers of second homes, who often wanted customized features that would have ratcheted up the price of our homes and disrupted our manufacturing schedule. Our rivals were better at providing higher-end homes than we, as a start-up, could have been. And frankly, I believed that there was more opportunity for growth in targeting first-time buyers—a quick look at the Census data told me there were more of them.

Once you know your customers, you can start to figure out what value you can provide them. In the early years of Kaufman and Broad, there was no way we could offer a customized house with a lot of frills because our customers couldn't afford one and we couldn't build one. But we could offer a great first home for a low price. Our defining goal would be to provide our customers the best product they could afford. That should be the guiding principle for most any company.

Many great companies have screwed this up. Steve Jobs's infamous Lisa computer cost too much to attract the business patrons Apple was trying to grab from other personal computer makers. In another failed product named for a relative, Ford's Edsel cars were priced so that they competed with Ford's existing products, confusing Ford customers and keeping others away from the brand. Always try to keep clearly in mind what your customers want and what you can offer.

And, I suppose, don't name things after your family members. You'll never be able to look at the product with a clear head.

To figure out what our customers could afford, we just had to look at their rent. When Kaufman and Broad started, owning a home meant being part of a neighborhood, establishing some stability, improving your credit, and achieving part of the American dream. No one was in the game of buying and selling homes quickly—what's called flipping today. Although a lot of people wanted to own a home, they generally weren't willing to overextend themselves to make the payments. (That came later, when bubbles deluded people into thinking real estate never goes down in value.) We decided to price our houses so that the mortgage payments would be less than the average monthly rent on an apartment. For many Americans, that remains the only way to make buying a home appealing, particularly after a market crash.

Focus on Value Because Your Customers Will

Value is one thing you never can afford to sacrifice.

Sometimes you have to go to extremes to reassure your customers that what you're selling really is worth what you're asking them to pay. Kaufman and Broad became the talk of the housing industry by doing just that when we hit our first major slowdown in the 1960s. The California housing market, one of our strongest through the middle of that decade, began contracting. Rather than lower our prices, we sold our customers a secure investment along with a place to live, demonstrating our confidence in our product, our company, and the economy.

In full-page newspaper ads, we made our customers an unprecedented (and, our competitors thought, quite unreasonable) offer: We guaranteed a roughly 7 percent increase in home value in the first year and offered to refund the difference to anyone who wanted to sell at the one-year mark. We promised to cover the mortgage payments for anyone who got laid off or was otherwise incapacitated. In other words, we reassured our customers that the new home they wanted really was a safe investment. And we made sure to assess our risk and to purchase insurance for ourselves beforehand in case our calculations were off.

Fortunately, they weren't. Buyers flocked to us, we never once had to make a mortgage payment, and our homes appreciated more than 7 percent. The downturn wasn't deep, it was just some jitters, as we had predicted through our research.

Market Like a Major Player, but Don't Spend Like One

SunAmerica was a tougher sell than Kaufman and Broad in several ways. Financial products were far more complicated than houses. Our market was national and our potential customers had a wider range of ages and incomes. Our competitors were enormous companies like Metropolitan, Prudential, and Hartford, which had a lot of customers, major name recognition, and ads with recognizable logos—the Peanuts characters, the Rock of Gibraltar, and the stag, respectively. Their marketing budgets were at least five times ours.

It seemed to us, though, that what mattered wasn't how much we spent but rather what sort of impact we made for our dollars. We leveraged what relatively little marketing money we had to make ourselves look as big as the big guys. We struck up a clever deal with NBC to brand a "SunAmerica NBC Sports Desk." Our logo and name would appear onscreen whenever the network's popular sports broadcasters were talking about world-class events such as Wimbledon and the Olympics. We maximized our screen time without having to pay for more than a few minutes of advertising. We thought of it as cost-effective vertical advertising.

Branding a sports desk is fairly typical now, but we were one of the first to do it. To have our name on the desk—on TV all the time and said aloud by respected and well-liked sportscasters—made us look like a much larger company. Our follow-up research with consumers showed that their recognition of our name had gone way up.

This sort of marketing—getting more for your money, looking bigger than you are—is great for a company that's just starting out. Frankly, you don't have much of a choice. But it's just as useful to keep in mind for a larger company. SunAmerica was at the height of its success in 1998, when we again leveraged our marketing budget.

We decided to advertise during the 1998 Super Bowl. We could have shelled out millions of dollars for one of those lavishly produced game time spots that have become the big advertising agencies' version of the Cannes Film Festival. Instead, we decided to advertise immediately before kickoff and immediately after the end of the game— times we knew that everyone would be watching. As far as customers could tell, we were Super Bowl advertisers, especially because our postgame ad aired before the trophy presentation. But we would spend a fraction of the money. In those days, a game time ad cost about $1.3 million; we got our spots for $250,000 each.

It turned out to be one of our smartest decisions for another reason. That year's Super Bowl was the famous contest between the Denver Broncos and the Green Bay Packers. Green Bay was the odds-on favorite to win, but with 2 minutes left in the game, the Broncos, led by their great quarterback, John Elway, scored and pulled into the lead. Those last 2 minutes leading into our commercial were the most watched of the game. We got more attention than we would have spending the extra million dollars to buy just one spot during the game. Packers fans were too shocked to touch the remote, and Denver backers were waiting for the replays. We reached them all.

MAKE WHAT YOU'RE SELLING MATTER—FROM THE NAME AND SLOGAN ON DOWN

Associating our product with sports worked because we were part of something our customers prized: their leisure. Starting with our first model home—the Award Winner—our company's sales pitch always appealed to our customers' basic yearning for a comfortable lifestyle. In Arizona we promised them that buying our sunny, low-priced homes with pools would let them "live like a movie star." We didn't exaggerate what our homes were—we didn't advertise mansions but build two-bedroom bungalows. We did, however, help our customers imagine what sort of life they could live in our homes: happy and fulfilling ones. We were selling a backdrop for the good life.

To give anyone a clear sense of how successful we were and how fast we moved, I came up with a great way to pitch our company. I made a calculation, based on how many houses we sold each year, and came up with the line that somebody bought a Kaufman and Broad home every 30 minutes of every working day. That thrilled share-holders, and customers knew they were buying from a strong company, not a fly-by-night operation. I repeated that line—as I do all my good lines—over and over until it caught on, until my employees said it, the press said it, and my investors said it. The line stuck not merely because it was catchy, but because it was true.

With our insurance business, we needed more than a slogan. Frankly, whoever decided to call it life insurance instead of death benefits was a marketing genius. But we wanted to move away from insurance altogether—it couldn't be part of our name or the way we thought of our company. We had to reimagine and retool our reason for being.

At first we hired a fancy corporate identity consultant to come up with a name for our new financial services company. After weeks of research, they informed us that the hot new trend was made-up company names with an x in them because customers thought the x seemed progressive. They came up with Abraxas. Exciting as it may have seemed to them, my head of marketing, Jana Greer, had the good sense to research the name and figure out it was also the title of a Carlos Santana album. (Imagine the licensing fees on that one.)

After all that fuss, it was Jana who finally came up with SunAmerica. I thought it was perfect. It dropped the word *insurance* from our title—because that wasn't all or even most of our business. We kept "Sun" for brand recognition and added "America" to give a sense of our nationwide scope.

With the name set, we devised our slogan. We researched and market-tested what gave people confidence in our skills and what showed our company's focus on its new mission. Then, we dubbed ourselves "The Retirement Specialist." Finally, we explained to our employees, our investors, and the press why we were going to be such a successful company. We were riding a major demographic wave by selling to baby boomers, the biggest and longest-living generation in American history, the products they would need for a happy and secure retirement.

It was far easier to sell our retirement savings products once we honed in on that segment of the industry. Because baby boomers were generally spenders and not savers, we rejected the typical ads with scenes of retirees playing golf, traveling, or relaxing with grandkids. Our most effective tagline, created with the number one ad agency at the time, Deutsch Inc., was "How will you spend your retirement?" Our ads featured luxury items like cars and diamond jewelry. We showed what those items cost and what a potential buyer would have in retirement savings if they invested the same amount in SunAmerica products—enough to ultimately buy the car and diamonds and to live comfortably in retirement. It was totally distinct from everyone else's advertising.

SELLING A CAUSE REQUIRES MORE THAN CONVICTION

Anytime someone is selling a cause, they often sit back and think they can sell on the merits alone. When I was raising money for the Museum of Contemporary Art and the Walt Disney Concert Hall, for instance, everyone thought that donors would simply see the value in having a museum and a new concert hall. But that wasn't enough.

To sell a cause, you have to rely on the same tactics as you would to sell a product—and the most important of these is a persuasive story that paints the big picture.

Selling Los Angeles is one of my favorite causes, and one of my hardest sells involved convincing the Democratic National Committee (DNC) to bring its 2000 convention to L.A.

The city's reputation had been steadily declining. The 1990s were a period marred by riots, fires, earthquakes, and the dispiriting O.J. Simpson trial—not to mention the dramatic decline of our local defense industry and the departure of many corporate headquarters in fields from banking to retailing. But we made the DNC understand that Los Angeles was on the rise and poised to be the city of the twenty-first century: a diverse metropolis embracing the emerging markets of Asia and Latin America and a place where new technologies were flourishing.

Even better, we promised to fund the convention almost entirely with private money. For decades, conventions had relied on taxpayer money, along with some individual donations. Ours would be the first to flip that equation. Unlike donations to political parties, donations to a convention would be tax deductible, which would help bring people on board. And we were sure that Democrats would take pride in saying their convention cost taxpayers very little money.

We also made sure the Democrats understood we were proposing a convention that would employ only union labor and whose volunteers would reflect the ethnic and gender diversity promoted by the party's values.

We got the convention.

Chapter 12

INVESTING

I can be an unreasonable investor because I can afford to take more risks.

Even so, I choose investments in the same methodical way I make business decisions: I start by doing my homework. When I'm unfamiliar with an investment category, I research and then develop a working thesis. As I read the newspapers each day, I am constantly processing and analyzing business developments, market movements, consumer trends, political shifts, and economic indicators.

My talented two-person investment team thought I had lost my marbles when I started to increase our position in gold in 2008. Gold, after all, is the favored investment of people who keep large stocks of canned goods and ammunition while scouting for signs of the apocalypse. At the time, though, I saw a series of events unfolding—the Fed lowered interest rates and injected liquidity into the market, which told me the dollar would decline and no other currency would be a viable option. Taken together, those things led me to believe that people would turn to gold. I increased our position from 1 percent to 5 percent of our holdings, and as our investment appreciated, it eventually increased to 15 percent, an allocation unheard of for any family investment office, any foundation, even most individual investors worth more than a billion. But I had a thesis and I stuck by it. From 2008 to 2011, gold increased from around $800 an ounce to more than $1,600 an ounce. My team didn't think I was so crazy—or even particularly unreasonable—then.

Don't Fear Risk, but Don't Take One if You Don't Have to

When assessing an investment, I look for what I like to call asymmetric opportunities, where my likelihood of earning a lot of money is higher than the risk of losing what I've put in.

Such opportunities don't come around often. Looking for assets that the market has underpriced, for whatever reason, can be an exhausting search. Recently, however, I found a prime one: A chance to purchase First Republic Bank.

Not long ago, First Republic was acquired by Merrill Lynch, which in turn was purchased by Bank of America. Bank of America needed some liquidity on its balance sheet, so it wanted to sell First Republic.

For me, the chance to participate in the purchase with private equity firms Colony Capital and General Atlantic was a no-brainer. Merrill had paid $1.8 billion for First Republic and now Bank of America was putting it on the block for about $1 billion. There was no need for lengthy analysis. I needed to know only a few things before I made a quick decision: what the valuation was, what type of bank it was, who was selling and why, the quality of the balance sheet, and how much influence we, as new owners, would have.

The bank had a very attractive valuation—priced at just one times book value. It was a healthy institution with a strong franchise in financial services, wealth management, and business banking. Bank of America also needed to raise money in a hurry, usually a clear signal of an asymmetric opportunity. Finally, our investor group would have a lot of influence because we would be a direct owner. That was it— I didn't need to look at every last financial statement.

First Republic was one of the largest investments we've ever made, and it paid off big. Some people would say it was irrational to invest major money in a bank so soon after the largest credit crisis in the nation's history, but I disagreed. Experience and instinct made me unreasonably confident that First Republic's niche serving

Eli Broad's parents, Rita and Leon Broad, were Lithuanian immigrants who instilled a solid work ethic in their only child. Leon ran a five-and-dime in Detroit, and Rita was a dressmaker.

Eli Broad graduated from high school in 1951 and, after graduating from Michigan State University in 1954, would go on to become the youngest certified public accountant in Michigan history.

Eli Broad proposed to Edythe "Edye" Lawson after only a few dates, promising her a comfortable life.

Eli and Edye Broad celebrated their 50th wedding anniversary in 2004. To mark the occasion, Eli underwrote an opera by Los Angeles Opera in Edye's honor, and Plácido Domingo sang at their anniversary party.

Eli and Edye Broad have two sons, Jeffrey (*far right*) and Gary (*far left*).

Eli Broad and Donald Kaufman started a homebuilding company in Detroit in 1957, offering homes without basements and with mortgage payments less than the rent for a two-bedroom apartment.

Eli Broad celebrates a company milestone. In 1961, Kaufman and Broad Home Corporation debuted as a public company on the American Stock Exchange and in 1969 went on to become the first home-builder on the New York Stock Exchange and a Fortune 500 company, today known as KB Home.

Kaufman and Broad's model homes drew first-time homebuyers eager to become homeowners. In its first year the company sold 120 homes and generated $1.7 million in revenue.

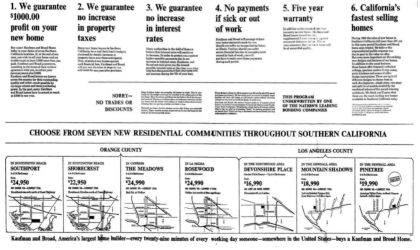

Kaufman and Broad did the unthinkable during an economic slowdown in the 1960s: They took out full-page ads guaranteeing their homes would appreciate and offering to make the mortgage payments for homebuyers who lost their jobs.

Workers in Los Angeles produce an assembly line of walls that will be trucked to a homebuilding site and erected by crane.

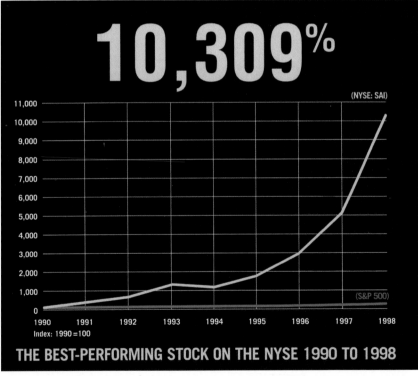

10,309%

(NYSE: SAI)

THE BEST-PERFORMING STOCK ON THE NYSE 1990 TO 1998

Index: 1990 = 100

Eli Broad transformed a traditional insurance company into the retirement savings powerhouse SunAmerica. The company was the best-performing stock on the New York Stock Exchange for nearly a decade. A $10,000 investment in Kaufman and Broad when it went public in 1961, including the shares of SunAmerica received in the spinoff, would have been worth $34.1 million when the company merged with AIG.

Eli Broad was the founding chairman of the Museum of Contemporary Art, created in 1979 by aggregating developer fees for public art to build the city's first contemporary art institution.

In one day Eli Broad negotiated the purchase of Count Giuseppe Panza di Biumo's remarkable collection of postwar American art for the Museum of Contemporary Art, giving the new museum a permanent collection. Broad and Panza are pictured here with their wives.

Robert Rauschenberg and Roy Lichtenstein are two of the artists featured in-depth in the Broad Collections.

Sculptor Richard Serra with Eli and Edye Broad and Joanne Heyler, director and chief curator of The Broad Art Foundation, after the installation of *No Problem* at the Broads' home.

The Frank Gehry–designed Walt Disney Concert Hall has become an iconic symbol of Los Angeles.
Source: Tom Bonner

Eli Broad celebrates the 2003 opening of Walt Disney Concert Hall with Los Angeles County Supervisor Zev Yaroslavsky, architect Frank Gehry, and campaign cochairs Andrea Van de Kamp and Los Angeles Mayor Richard Riordan.

Eli Broad led the successful campaign to bring the 2000 Democratic National Convention to Los Angeles. He shares the victory with Los Angeles Mayor Richard Riordan and California Governor Gray Davis.

Eli Broad and Los Angeles Mayor Antonio Villaraigosa discuss plans for the Grand Avenue Project, a $2 billion redevelopment of the city's downtown arts, civic, and cultural district.

Alan Cranston asked Eli Broad to chair his U.S. Senate campaign in 1968, giving Broad his first experience in fund-raising.

Jeff Koons has become one of Eli and Edye Broad's dearest friends and most treasured artists in their collections. The Broad Collections have 27 works by the artist.

For the purchase of Jeff Koons's iconic *Balloon Dog*, Eli Broad did something he had never done before: pay in full for a work not yet fabricated. The sculpture has been exhibited at museums including the Los Angeles County Museum of Art; the Museum of Fine Arts, Boston; the Guggenheim in Bilbao, Spain; and the Corcoran Gallery of Art in Washington, D.C.

Source: Jeff Koons, Balloon Dog (Blue), *1994–2000, high chromium stainless steel with transparent color coating, 121 × 143 × 45 inches, © Jeff Koons. Installation view of Jeff Koons's* Balloon Dog (Blue), *1994–2001, at the Museum of Fine Arts, Boston. Collection of The Broad Art Foundation, Santa Monica, California. Photograph © 2006 Museum of Fine Arts, Boston.*

Architect Renzo Piano and Eli Broad review plans for The Broad Contemporary Art Museum at the Los Angeles County Museum of Art as curator Joanne Heyler looks on.

Eli Broad's insistence on maximizing gallery space in The Broad Contemporary Art Museum resulted in an unconventional approach to design. By moving the stairs to the exterior of the building, Renzo Piano designed an efficient building with 90 percent of its space devoted to galleries.
Source: © Weldon Brewster

Eli and Edye Broad unveil the design for The Broad, their new museum on Grand Avenue in downtown Los Angeles.

Eli Broad discusses plans for The Broad with architect Liz Diller. The new contemporary art museum and headquarters for The Broad Art Foundation will open in early 2014.

Eli and Edye Broad announce their $100 million gift to create The Broad Institute. Harvard and the Massachusetts Institute of Technology (MIT) matched the gift to become partners in the new genomic medicine institute. Pictured with the Broads are MIT President Charles M. Vest, Whitehead Institute Director Susan Lindquist, Broad Institute Director Eric Lander, and Harvard University President Larry Summers.

Today, The Broad Institute has more than 1,900 researchers and a $258 million budget. The Broads have given $600 million to the institute, which they believe will improve human health worldwide.
Source: Len Rubenstein

Now on his fourth career, Eli Broad believes his philanthropic work in restoring America's public schools to international greatness is vital for a strong middle class, a healthy economy, and a vibrant democracy.

Eli Broad announces that the New York City Department of Education wins the 2007 Broad Prize for Urban Education, as U.S. Secretary of Education Margaret Spellings watches Chancellor Joel Klein celebrate with Randi Weingarten, president of the United Federation of Teachers.

Eli and Edye Broad meet the 2007 cohort of The Broad Residency, a two-year program to infuse talented managers into K–12 public education. More than 250 Broad Residents are working in public school systems, charter management organizations, and state and federal departments of education.

Eli Broad endowed the college of business and graduate school of management at Michigan State University, his alma mater.

Eli Broad has been behind some of the most architecturally significant public institutions, including (starting from top left) The Broad Center for the Biological Sciences at Caltech by Pei Cobb Freed & Partners Architects, The Broad Art Center at the University of California, Los Angeles, by Richard Meier, the Caltrans District 7 Headquarters by Thom Mayne, The Broad Center of Regeneration Medicine and Stem Cell Research at the University of California, San Francisco, by Rafael Viñoly, the High School for the Visual and Performing Arts by Wolf Prix, and The Broad Art Museum at Michigan State University by Zaha Hadid.

Over the course of his six-decade career in business and philanthropy, Eli Broad has met and worked with Presidents Nixon, Carter, Reagan, Clinton, Bush, and Obama.

higher-income customers would continue to grow, and I knew we had the opportunity to make good money. Under the worst outcome, we still would recoup our investment. In five months the bank went public at a significant premium to book value, and we ended up doubling our money in about a year.

Opportunities like that aren't available to everyone. My wealth gives me access to investments most people don't have.

Focus on Picking an Advisor, Not Stocks

When I'm asked the question "How should I invest my money?" I give an answer that isn't very satisfying to most people: Don't invest your money yourself. Hire a professional to do it for you.

Most people don't have the time or the expertise to be a successful investor. Unless you're willing to put in the 24/7 sort of diligence that a professional investor does, don't try to pick your own stocks or other investments. Nothing can get you into more trouble than occasionally dabbling in the market. You would be surprised how few billionaires do much day-to-day investing. I have employed a talented two-person investment team for more than a decade, and they research, advise, and execute.

What matters, though, is that you do invest your money. You can't save your way to wealth. When I grew up, only a small minority of Americans were investors. Prudent people, like my parents, counted on a lifetime's savings, Social Security, and in many cases, an employer-funded defined benefit pension plan to carry them through retirement. That's all changed.

Today, you have to take more risk per dollar to get a decent rate of return. There is no passive way to make your hard-earned money grow. The lowest-risk savings instruments—such as certificates of deposit, municipal bonds, or Treasuries—are paying historically low rates of return. With fewer workers and more retirees every year, Social Security faces collapse when current deposits aren't enough to cover retirement payments. If you're like most American employees, your company has replaced its defined benefit pension with a 401(k) retirement savings plan. Take advantage of that. If you're under 50, the government will let you shield a maximum of $17,000 of your gross salary from taxes if you put it in your 401(k). If you're over 50, you can sock away up to $22,500 pretax. No matter your age, your employer will likely match at least some of what you save. Though the contribution limits and employer matching amounts may change year to year, it's still free money.

A good financial advisor will create an investment strategy that, ideally, combines a diversified portfolio of investment vehicles and takes into account how much you have to invest, what your goals and timeline are, and your willingness to take risk. To find the best advisor, ask friends and relatives for recommendations or consult with reputable firms like Charles Schwab. When you identify one or two advisors, make sure you ask for several references you can call. Picking a good financial advisor will be the most important investment decision you make.

If you insist on directing your own investments, I recommend that you buy quality, low-cost mutual funds through firms like Vanguard or Fidelity. Some of their funds will let you set a target retirement date and the fund will adjust your asset allocations into lower-risk instruments as that date approaches, taking the guesswork out of saving for the future.

As you consider different asset classes, let me plug annuities and suggest you discuss them with your advisor. I've had annuities in my portfolio since the first days SunAmerica pioneered the tax-deferred savings vehicles. Variable annuities let you make payments or deposit a lump sum, which you then invest, usually in a range of mutual funds. Your ultimate return is determined by how well your investments do. They are attractive instruments because they allow the holder to adjust the asset allocation as frequently as necessary—all without paying taxes.

I first bought annuities from SunAmerica, but then I switched to Vanguard because their fees were lower and I didn't need the financial planning advice SunAmerica offered. You should always consider taxes and fees when you're selecting investment vehicles—and make sure you ask your financial advisor about the tax and fee implications—because they will reduce the amount of money you keep from your investment returns.

DIVERSIFY OR DIE

In addition to a reasonable fee structure, you want to make sure your financial advisor maintains a diversified portfolio.

I didn't follow my own advice on diversification until I stepped away from the day-to-day management of SunAmerica after our merger with AIG. Virtually my entire net worth was tied up in our companies because I knew every detail of their financial health. It was the best investment I could make at the time. But when I left the company I wanted to diversify and sell some of my shares. That didn't sit well with AIG CEO Hank Greenberg, so I left the board in 2005. Shortly thereafter, I went from having more than 80 percent of my net worth in AIG to about 10 percent.

In investing, as in life, it's sometimes better to be lucky than smart. I never saw the precipitous fall of AIG coming—and to this day, it troubles me that a legendary company could drop in value as it did in 2008. Fortunately, our foundations had none of their funds in AIG.

These days I am highly diversified. Name an asset class and I probably have some exposure to it. Between my portfolio and that of the foundations, we have more than 200 investments, none of which amounts to more than 5 percent of our holdings.

VOLATILITY HAPPENS

Diversification helps ease the pain of a volatile market, when losses are inevitable.

Conventional wisdom suggests that investors should wait around for a certain return—like doubling or tripling their money with a particular investment. As a consequence, people end up selling their best stocks and holding on to their losers. Lots of investors follow the sell-it-when-it-doubles rule and miss the multiplier that comes from holding a great performing investment for a substantial period.

One of the toughest losses I have ever taken was during AIG's liquidity crisis and bailout in the general financial meltdown of 2008. I had sold all but a small percentage of my AIG stock a few years prior to the crash, but I watched in disbelief as the value of my remaining stock plummeted on September 15, 2008, when Lehman Brothers filed for bankruptcy and AIG accepted a bailout from the U.S. government. But as soon as prices bumped up a bit in 2009, and I concluded that any further recovery could take years, I sold without emotion, keeping just my stock options, which I couldn't exercise.

I have lived through a lot of recessions, but that year was probably the toughest crisis I've seen. Even so, I tried very hard not to become emotional and I took ownership of all my decisions. There's always money to be made somewhere in the market if you have a balanced portfolio and maintain some liquidity.

Accept that volatility happens. There's no formula for avoiding it, and there's no way to predict it. The only thing to do is maintain the long view of your investments and make sure your investment advisor is doing the same. It's tempting to want to check your portfolio when the market dips or spikes and to react in an emotional, knee-jerk fashion. But if you invest, you will lose money from time to time. Learn from a loss, but don't take it to heart. Equally important, don't fall in love with any particular company or fund for any reason apart from performance. If you decide to sell, do it and don't look back. Think of yourself as somebody with an eye on the future and a mind educated by the past.

Chapter 13

NEGOTIATION

My first negotiation was with a landlord.

He was a high school principal in East Lansing, Michigan, and he had rented his house, a comfortable two-story colonial, to me and some college friends for the summer. He was going on vacation, and we were going to summer school.

None of us had ever lived in our own house before. We soon figured out that the best thing to do with that much space was to throw parties. They started out small, but as word got around, they grew. By midsummer, our guests even included members of the Michigan State football team. I was a big football fan, and Michigan State was just starting a long winning streak, so I didn't mind that one bit—until the night a beefy lineman decided to body slam our landlord's baby grand piano, taking one of its legs right off.

A week later, the landlord decided to interrupt his upstate holiday to pay us a surprise visit.

The house was not a pretty sight. Our landlord was understandably upset. He took one look at his damaged piano and started shouting that he would call Michigan State's dean and have us all expelled. My roommates were struck dumb with fear.

I knew I had to step in. Mustering my nerve, I told our landlord he had two choices: He could throw us out of his house and get us kicked out of school, which meant he'd have to take care of the mess and repairs himself and find new tenants, or he could forgo calling the dean and let us clean up the house and pay to repair the piano.

He mulled over my offer for what seemed like ages. Finally, he shrugged his shoulders and said, "Fine." With that, he returned to his vacation. My roommates sighed with relief. We were on the hook for a few hundred bucks, but that was nothing compared to expulsion from school.

I had successfully concluded my first negotiation because I had done three things: made a fair offer, kept my emotions under control, and taken the other party's interests into account. I improvised that day with the landlord, but with a little forethought and self-discipline, you can apply these three rules to negotiations in every field.

How to Make a Sound Offer Every Time

Negotiation is something many people dread, but believe it or not, it can be pretty simple. I have a formula for making an offer, and once you learn it, you can put it to work in a host of situations.

Let's say it's springtime and your house could use some window washing after a wet winter. So you call the first company listed online and they come over and give you a quote. Most people would just accept the estimate or, at most, call up a few other companies and pick the one with the lowest price. Assuming the bidders all are equally competent, why not start with the lowest price and negotiate for a better one?

All you have to do is make the following calculation: What supplies are needed at what cost? How many workers and hours are required to do the job? Factor in wages for the workers, a decent sum for the company's overhead, and a fair profit for the owner. That's it—costs, overhead, and profit.

The sum of those things is your offer. Stick to it, and you've followed the first rule of negotiation.

In a Good Negotiation, Everybody Wins

Fairness is the most essential part of any negotiation. Over the years, people have said a lot of things about my negotiating style—that I'm tough or that I always get what I want. But they can't honestly say I'm unfair.

If you're unfair, people won't want to do business with you again.

Let's go back to those window washers. Generally, the difference between their quotes will reflect the differences in the profit they're hoping to make. Some may pay their workers a little more or buy costlier supplies, but most of the difference will be in their projected profit.

Never try to negotiate the profit down to zero or even below what's reasonable. A successful negotiation isn't about you getting everything you want and the other guy getting nothing. In the ideal negotiation, both parties should emerge feeling like they've won— maybe not everything they wanted, but something. Fair negotiations can be the beginning of a relationship, often a long-lasting one.

Never Be Afraid to Ask

The most valuable research actually can occur during the negotiation itself. Don't be afraid to ask questions—I always do. Ask the window washing company how many employees they use per job and what supplies they need. Maybe ask for the time it takes to do one window so that you can multiply by the number of windows you have. Chances are, they'll just think you're curious.

Once you have the information and have done the calculation, you can feel confident in your offer, which will help you stick to it. You're not trying to gouge the other person. You're trying to create a situation in which you pay a fair price and he makes a fair profit.

You can apply this formula for making an offer to pretty much anything you're negotiating—not to mention all the things you think can't be bargained over. Apply it to all your home maintenance—painting, carpet cleaning, roofing, tiling, landscaping, plumbing—and to buying a house or car. Sometimes people will say flat out, no negotiation—in fact, at Kaufman and Broad, we made sure not to let our buyers bargain or pick and choose options because standardization was the only way we could offer homes at a low price. But if the other party doesn't say that up front, it's an open field. There's never any harm in trying.

The last question I always like to ask, when I've asked all the rest and we've had a back-and-forth but I'm not quite happy with my negotiating partner's last offer, is this: "Is that the best you can do?" In another context, it's a question I also ask my employees, as you'll see in Chapter 16. But it works wonders in a negotiation. You'd be surprised how many times it makes the other person say, "Let me think about it" or "Let me do the numbers again," before they lower the price.

If this sounds simple, that's because it is. Trust me. The hard part is when emotions threaten to cloud everyone's head.

Surviving the Silences and the Stares—Stay Unemotional and Disciplined

One of the reasons most people dislike negotiation is that it involves confrontation. You have to stand your ground and react to pushback. Whether you're negotiating with your gardener about how much he'll charge to trim your trees or with an auto dealer about the sales price of a used car, most people feel uncomfortable with the back-and-forth and are nervous about starting the process at all.

That's when you need to take a deep breath and remember the second of the three rules I outlined: keep control of your emotions. Getting emotional is the quickest way to botch a negotiation. You'll either push too hard—making the other party feel bullied or unfairly treated—or you'll give in too soon because you're afraid to stick to your guns.

The way to avoid getting emotional is to exercise discipline before you enter a negotiation. First, set your limit. What's the most you're willing to pay or the least you're willing to work for? If the other party pushes you beyond the number you've set for yourself, be prepared to walk away.

My limit is always firm at the most I think something is worth. I never pay more. That hasn't changed from when I was 23 and had a few hundred bucks to my name. Early in my career, I never would have imagined I would pay tens of millions of dollars for a piece of art. But I've loosened up a bit, and I understand that if you love something, its value is calculated in more than dollars.

Take a sculpture I bought in 2005, David Smith's *Cubi XXVIII*. Many people consider Smith, who was part of the abstract expressionist circle, to be the twentieth century's preeminent American sculptor. I had wanted a *Cubi* since 1994, when one came up for auction at Sotheby's. When the price went above $4 million—too high by my estimate—I dropped out. As the years passed, I regretted it. Smith made only 28 of the towering stainless steel pieces, and all but three already were in museums. I had underestimated both the piece's rarity and the escalation in prices the contemporary art market would undergo. In 2005, when another *Cubi* came up for auction, I was determined to get it. Even so, I maintained my discipline and went into the sales room with a top price—$25 million—in my head. I got the piece for $23.8 million, which was the highest price ever paid at the time for a contemporary work of art at auction.

Whenever you're going into a negotiation, recognize how badly you want something and what you're willing to do to get it—even pay a premium, a price higher than what others might pay or think it's worth. But make that calculation before you are in the heat of negotiation. Then be disciplined. Never let emotion or exhaustion or anything else lure you beyond that limit.

BE READY TO SAY YES AND DON'T SIT DOWN UNLESS YOU CAN MAKE A DECISION

If you enter a negotiation without having the power to say yes or no—if you need to run things by colleagues or bosses or lawyers or accountants—you risk losing whatever ground you've gained. You risk having to start again, maybe at a different and more difficult place once your negotiating partner has had time to think. Don't go into the room unless you're prepared to make a decision.

In my negotiation to buy an important art collection for the Museum of Contemporary Art, for instance, I made sure not to start talks until I had the go-ahead from MOCA's full board.

MOCA was a brand-new institution in a city that previously had lacked a showcase for contemporary art. We had a building, a board, and an endowment—but no art. That was a problem for an art museum.

One of our trustees, Count Giuseppe Panza di Biumo, was facing a problem in that he had to sell his great collection of contemporary art—80 works amassed between 1956 and 1963—or pay enormous taxes on it, which he could not afford. The count, an Italian businessman and one of the first European collectors of American postwar art, was upset. He had spent decades studying art, meeting artists, and painstakingly acquiring first-rate artworks. He was a smart collector with a great eye, and all his work would be for nothing if the collection was broken up and sold to private collectors around the world. If he couldn't have them, he wanted to see them all in a good public museum.

The count's collection was perfect for MOCA. It contained works by Mark Rothko, Robert Rauschenberg, Franz Kline, Roy Lichtenstein, and several other leading artists. The pieces the count had were all stellar examples of those artists' work. Sotheby's appraised the collection at somewhere between $11 million and $15 million. MOCA's board decided the highest we could afford to pay was $12 million. I decided to start negotiations at $11 million—a fair point because it was Sotheby's low estimate—and I aimed to stay at that price, although I was willing to negotiate other particulars.

I spent about six months wooing the count—showing him around L.A., introducing him to our then mayor, Tom Bradley, and making sure he saw why the city needed his collection. But the actual negotiations were completed in a day. That's because the MOCA board had already given me its limit and had given me full authority to negotiate and to sign a deal. The timing was right too—the count had to sell soon because the Italian government had given him a deadline that was approaching.

DON'T SWING WILDLY—START CLOSE TO WHERE YOU WANT TO END UP

In negotiations a lot of people like to start very low and work their way to the middle. They think this makes both parties happy—the feeling of winning ground, of coming to agreement from a great distance.

I disagree. Going back-and-forth wastes too much time, and more often than not, people feel like they're losing each round rather than winning.

Instead, I do something that most people consider unreasonable: I make a first offer that's pretty close to my final offer. I leave a little wiggle room, some space to meet the other party, but that's it. This shocks people and makes them think I drive a hard bargain. In fact, I'm just saying exactly what I mean and sticking to it. Most people will meet my offer, or come very close, once they realize I'm not going to budge much from what we both know is fair. It saves us all a lot of time and pain.

In my MOCA negotiation with the count, my first offer was almost precisely where I wanted to end up—even though my limit was a bit higher. I stuck to $11 million, although the count pushed for $12 million. I countered by promising him a higher down payment. We were able to agree on $11 million with the higher down. The collection today is probably worth at least a billion dollars.

I was able to keep my head, not get emotional, and stick to my offer when the count made his counterproposal. Knowing you've made a fair offer, setting your limit, and keeping a level head should prevent you from doubting your position, no matter what. You'll have to face counteroffers, dead silence, steely gazes, and awkward pauses. But you have to keep your eye on the endgame and not let all the rest distract you.

NEVER FORGET WHAT MAKES THE OTHER GUY TICK

The third rule of negotiation is to be conscious of the other person's motives. These include the things he or she tells you up front, extenuating circumstances you know about the person, and what you determine is important to the person with whom you're negotiating. Those latter factors can be the most powerful.

For my negotiation with the count, I knew his interests from the start. He often visited L.A. in his capacity as a MOCA trustee and to check out the local art scene. He stayed at our guesthouse with his wife. When it came time to sell his collection, I knew his foremost concerns: Selling soon to avoid paying taxes and keeping his collection whole rather than seeing it dispersed piece by piece.

I worked all this into my offer by promising the count we would be a very swift buyer and by assuring him we would try our hardest to keep the collection whole—that we would sell a piece only if we needed the money to pay him.

I also thought about issues that the count hadn't articulated but I could reasonably assume were on his mind. Because he was a MOCA trustee, I figured he would like to have a hand in ensuring the museum became a world-class institution—which it instantly would if we had his collection. I knew he liked Los Angeles because he loved its artists, particularly Robert Irwin and James Turrell. And I knew he would like the idea of keeping his collection together.

But the best move you can make in a negotiation is to think of an incentive the other person hasn't even thought of—and then meet it. That's what sealed my negotiation with the count, and it occurred to me only when I was sitting opposite him.

He was pushing for $12 million, and I wanted to stick to $11 million. I offered him a higher down payment with the balance paid out over several years. The count agreed but wanted more money up front.

That's when it came to me. If we gave the count an even bigger lump-sum payment up front, he would have to convert it to Italian lira. Going from dollars to lira was a losing proposition. The lira was inflating fast. If he converted more right away, he would end up with less money than if we paid him some now and some later.

If you can find an incentive like this—something the other party hasn't yet figured out—it can change the tenor of your negotiation. It will immediately be clear to them that you're not trying to trick or manipulate them and that you just want everyone to get a fair deal. It's the most powerful tool in any negotiator's bag. To use it, of course, you have to do a lot of homework.

When I shared my thinking on the lira, the count agreed with my initial offer. I had managed to see an incentive he had missed. In doing so, I helped him actually make more money, without losing anything for the museum. We were both winners—and the biggest winners of all were MOCA and the city of Los Angeles.

Now that's negotiating.

Chapter 14

THE LOGIC OF BEING LOGICAL

I'm unreasonably logical.

I don't mean I'm irrational—because that's something you never want to be. Rather, logic is when you look at all the facts and they lead you to the conclusion that something makes sense.

And unreasonable logic is when you stick to facts and sensible conclusions when others are giving in to emotion or distraction.

One of the areas where that has been particularly helpful is in our foundation's support of biomedical research. Over time I had become convinced that our family's philanthropy ought to approach medical research the way a venture capitalist approaches investment—look for promising new ideas and put up seed money that can be leveraged. It's a concept that produced exceptional results when we got involved in creating a genomic research institute in 2001.

For years one of our sons had suffered from Crohn's disease, which has no known cause or cure. As a parent you never want to see your child suffer, and Edye and I were beyond frustrated with our inability to help. We decided to start The Broad Medical Research Program to fund small seed grants for PhDs and other nontraditional researchers doing innovative and early-stage research into inflammatory bowel disease, which includes Crohn's and ulcerative colitis. Their work, however innovative and ambitious, generally wasn't far enough along to qualify for traditional funding sources such as the National Institutes of Health. One of our early grantees was Eric Lander, who was working to decode the human genome and studying a gene related to Crohn's disease at the Whitehead Institute at the Massachusetts Institute of Technology.

In October 2001, when Edye and I were in Cambridge for my induction into the American Academy of Arts and Sciences, we called Eric and asked to see his lab. He's an impressive researcher with an eclectic and high-achieving background: a math PhD from Oxford, where he was a Rhodes Scholar, and a professorship in managerial economics at the Harvard Business School. When we visited him, we saw an ideal work environment, packed with young scientists and humming with the sound of robotics. The scientists were working on the weekend because they loved what they were doing. It seemed like no one wanted to go home.

We asked Eric how long his work would take and what he planned to do when he was finished decoding the human genome. We were fascinated when he told us about his idea to start an inter-disciplinary institute to take what he had learned about the genome to bedside application—so it would benefit patients by helping to treat and even prevent disease. Eric had a vision for a new way of conducting science, breaking down the silos that usually keep medical researchers, biologists, and engineers from collaborating on common projects. I was intrigued, but when Eric told us he needed $800 million to start it, I just wished him luck.

Still, I couldn't stop thinking about the prospect of creating a new sort of institution whose work could make such a difference in the lives of so many.

Some of my initial inclinations were emotionally rather than logically based. I thought such an institute ought to be in our hometown, Los Angeles, as a joint effort of USC, UCLA, and the California Institute of Technology (Caltech)—where I was on the board and close to its then president, the Nobel Laureate David Baltimore. But Eric wanted it in Cambridge because, as he logically argued, moving everything to the West Coast would be extremely costly and would add several years to the project.

We talked about creating a partnership between MIT, which operated the Whitehead Institute, where Eric worked, and Harvard University. That would be a problem. The two schools never had collaborated on anything—let alone an enormous, cutting-edge research institute—and it was unclear whether they could be convinced to work together. Their students and staff were too accustomed to thinking of each other as competitors.

However, they also were a group for whom logic was likely to be persuasive.

A Logical Idea Is One That Makes You Say, "Why Didn't I Think of That?"

The logic of our idea for a new scientific institute was clear to anyone with an open mind. I proposed that Edye and I put up $100 million in seed money over 10 years, provided Harvard and MIT would come up with matching sums.

The next step was to meet the presidents of both universities. MIT saw the potential and was on board almost immediately, but then Harvard President Larry Summers told us initially that Harvard didn't have the money.

After the meeting, Eric and I agreed that, despite whatever Larry said, there was no way Harvard would want to be left out of something so big, an institute that would draw talent and attention from around the world. That appeal to Harvard's self-interest was our leverage—and we were right. Today, the institute is a powerhouse in the vital field of basic biomedical research. Edye and I believe so strongly in the institute's potential for improving human health—and were so impressed by its early work— that we put up a second $100 million two years after the institute got off the ground and $400 million three years later for an endowment.

The Broad Institute had a logical clarity. Eric wanted to take the knowledge from decoding the human genome and apply it to treating and even preventing disease. He wanted to make all of The Broad Institute's discoveries available for free online to further advance research worldwide. And most of all, he wanted to create a new way of conducting science, thus revolutionizing medical research. With Eric's leadership, the institute we helped MIT and Harvard create is accomplishing exactly these goals.

LIKE WINE, AN IDEA MAY NEED TO AGE

Sometimes you'll have to admit that there are things even sound logic can't overcome. I've encountered a few of those while attempting to help turn Los Angeles's Grand Avenue into the region's primary civic and cultural district.

Ever since our family moved to Los Angeles in 1963, I've heard complaints—make that sneers—about L.A. lacking a center. Heck, when I wanted to move our business to L.A. in 1960, I found the place too physically confusing and initially opted for Phoenix instead.

People have been trying to rebuild L.A.'s downtown since it slipped into decay in the years after World War II. By the late 1960s, the city had razed the Victorian homes and boarding houses on historic Bunker Hill. Development happened piecemeal, leaving much of what could have been a great pedestrian boulevard looking like a desert highway. The city's main concourse remained Wilshire Boulevard, which was the world's first great processional avenue designed with the automobile specifically in mind. That meant parking lots behind buildings, entrances from the parking lot rather than from the sidewalk, and big windows with displays made for viewing by drivers, not pedestrians. L.A. pushed west, developing along Wilshire, and just kept on going. Downtown grew increasingly desolate.

While working on Disney Hall, I began to see how badly downtown needed smart development. That's also when I realized how hard it would be to do. The parcels along Grand Avenue were owned separately by the county and the city, and those governments had never come together to develop an overall plan.

But the logical thing to do was exactly that, to make something cohesive and centered. I knew it would need businesses, retail, restaurants, housing, and inviting spaces to gather and for pedestrians to walk.

We had to convince the city and county to work together by creating an entirely new administrative structure to cut through the bureaucracy. We started by creating the Grand Avenue Committee, a public-private partnership of civic leaders, developers, and urban planners, with real estate developer Jim Thomas and me serving as co-chairs. After a dozen drafts of by-laws and a lot of negotiation, the city, county, and Community Redevelopment Agency agreed to form the Joint Powers Authority, composed of city, county, and state officials. The JPA, in turn, charged the Grand Avenue Committee with finding a financially sound and cooperative developer that would bring to life the vision of Grand Avenue as a vibrant center of our region of 15 million people. The nine-acre, $2 billion development would include 3.6 million square feet of development, 450,000 square feet of retail, a 16-acre park, a 275-room luxury hotel and up to 2,600 residential units. We found an ideal partner in the Related Companies, best known for building Time Warner Center in Manhattan. We needed to make sure Related had skin in the game so they couldn't walk. I gave them this unreasonable request without budging: If they wanted to be our developer, they had to put $50 million down. Nobody thought they would agree, but they did—because I stuck to my guns, didn't get emotional, and reminded them that $50 million was a tiny fraction of the project's $2 billion price tag.

Unfortunately, a crashing economy trumped logic. For years, the project has been delayed. But Related has been a strong partner throughout, and thanks to that deposit money and interest, the city has started the first phase of the Grand Avenue Project: the construction of a civic park from City Hall to the Music Center, set to open in the summer of 2012.

Sometimes logic dictates that the moment for a good idea hasn't quite arrived. If that happens, move on to the next thing, bide your time, and return to your idea when the time is right. Patience can be the most logical course.

Chapter 15

I Ain't Nothing but
a Hound Dog

People who work with me know that one of my mottos is: be a hound dog, not a kennel dog.

I adopted this saying when I was in my early 20s from a legendary chairman of General Motors, Charles Wilson, who ran that company in its postwar heyday. He was in charge of GM during the winter of my freshman year of college, when I was a drill press operator and United Auto Workers member at a rival company, Packard. (This was the latest in my string of random jobs, along with selling women's shoes and garbage disposals.)

Wilson made his comment about hound dogs and kennel dogs after President Dwight Eisenhower had appointed him secretary of defense. It was not Wilson's finest moment. He used the line to explain why he opposed assistance to the unemployed—because he said they would, like kennel dogs, always wait for scraps rather than going on the hunt.

A lot of people shook their heads at that heartless application of a good metaphor, including me. But I've thought his words clearly applied to entrepreneurs or anyone with some ambition. You can't wait for opportunities to come to you. Instead, go hunting.

Go After Big Game

I'm unreasonably persistent, so the hard work it takes to be a hound dog comes naturally to me. I never let up until I get what I want—or until the logic of the situation makes it clear my goal really is out of reach. This means I win big and I lose big. There's no middle ground; a hound never settles for scraps.

In the 1980s I went on one of my biggest hunts. Kaufman and Broad had bought the Sun Life Insurance Company a decade earlier, and I was ready to make some acquisitions to build it up. I set my sights on a company called Baldwin United.

I came across the story of Baldwin in the news, always your best source of information. As I mentioned in Chapter 4, I read four newspapers a day. To this day I get many of my ideas from sources available to anyone who takes the time to read and think through the implications of what's on the page. If you make a habit of it, you may be fortunate enough to develop a kind of sixth sense for the opportunities embedded in public events—something like the hound dog's sense of smell.

Baldwin, believe it or not, was a piano seller turned financial services company. That diversification did not go well. Baldwin filed a $9 billion bankruptcy, the biggest ever in those innocent days long before the 2008 collapse of Lehman Brothers. Six insurance companies that had sold annuities—valued at about $4 billion—to Baldwin's 165,000 policyholders were located in Indiana and Arkansas. The insurance commissioners in those states seized all six companies and then began looking for the right suitor to take them over.

As soon as I expressed an interest in pursuing Baldwin assets, however, people pointed out that our competitor would be Metropolitan Life, an insurance industry titan that, at one time, had insured one out of every five Americans. It was the company that financed construction of the Empire State Building and helped carry the country through World War II by investing its assets in war bonds. If we were hounds, they were winners of the Westminster Kennel Club show— but I'll back hunger over pedigree every time.

It's important not to let conventional wisdom set the limit on your ambition. Being unreasonably ambitious will push you to do more and be more than even you may imagine you can be. It's what made me believe we could compete with Metropolitan for those annuities—no matter what anyone else thought.

WHETHER OR NOT YOU SUCCEED, YOU HAVE TO KEEP HUNTING

I thought we had done all the right things in our attempt to take over Baldwin's policies—getting organized, lining up allies, putting together a great pitch, negotiating firmly and without emotion. Thanks to my friend Mickey Kantor, whom I met through Alan Cranston, I even got the backing of Arkansas's ambitious young governor, Bill Clinton. We hired powerful bankers and lawyers based in that state—a prerequisite for doing business there. Most significant, or so I believed, we promised a 2-point-higher interest rate for Baldwin annuity holders than Metropolitan put on the table. Our offer required the insurance commissioners to respond within 10 days. They didn't meet the deadline, and we didn't budge. Metropolitan won the first round, but that didn't mean I was about to give up the chase for the long-term rights to administer those annuities.

Over the next few months, Kaufman and Broad pulled out all the stops. We advertised on billboards and radio stations in the cities where Baldwin's subsidiaries did business. We wrote to every insurance commissioner in the country and held press conferences touting the benefits of our offer. We came on so strong that Metropolitan, the giant, actually got worried. They launched their own advertising campaign and press offensive. We went at it in the papers—talking up our plans and our companies.

In the end, Metropolitan won, although they couldn't meet the rates they eventually promised. At first blush, it looked like we had spent a lot of time and money for nothing, a dead loss. But the thing about falling short of an unreasonable ambition is that there's often an upside.

In this case, our apparently fruitless quest enhanced our company's image. Before we started vying for Baldwin, few people had ever heard of Sun Life, even though it had been around for a century. All of a sudden, we were all over the press, Sun Life's David battling toe-to-toe with Met Life's Goliath. Soon the "little guy" image was discarded and we were being mentioned in the same breath as Met's competitors. Everyone sat up and took notice.

UNREASONABLE PERSISTENCE PRODUCES BIG PAYOFFS

One of the lessons I took away from the struggle over Baldwin was that big ambition requires big action and all the advocates you can get, especially when business and politics intersect, as they often do. After our Baldwin struggle was over, then Governor Clinton told me that we hadn't gotten what we wanted in Arkansas because the insurance commissioner was predisposed in Metropolitan's favor. (Not long after, he joined the law firm that represented Met.) In short order, I realized that the lessons I shared with you in the chapters on negotiation and leverage were just as applicable to politics, though in politics, you often have to be a lot more persistent.

Persistence was the key to breaking ground on The Broad, the future home of our family and foundation art collections. After we announced our intention to build the museum, three years of negotiation and maneuvering followed. Our first choice was downtown Los Angeles, but the developer of the Grand Avenue Project was trying to woo the Motion Picture Academy of Arts and Sciences to build a museum downtown, so we looked elsewhere. We considered sites in Santa Monica and in Beverly Hills, both of which courted us. That gave us valuable leverage when L.A. Mayor Antonio Villaraigosa called and asked us to consider a spot on Grand Avenue across from Disney Hall. In the intervening years, the Grand Avenue Project had stalled because of the poor economy. The developer was willing to abandon its plans to build a condo tower across from Disney Hall in favor of letting us build a museum to jump-start the effort.

I had always thought our museum belonged on Grand Avenue. But building there meant dealing with the city and the county—both of which had jurisdiction over the site—and L.A.'s Community Redevelopment Agency. Maneuvering among multiple government agencies seemed like a lot, but I thought, "Why not?"

The part that required the most persistence was getting the entire Los Angeles County Board of Supervisors to support us. Los Angeles County is America's largest local government unit, and the five elected supervisors exercise both legislative and executive power. Some of the supervisors were unhappy that the development agreement would allow us to lease the land for $1 a year, a common concession to cultural institutions in L.A. and other cities. This upset the supervisors even though they had already ceded the same to the developer of the overall Grand Avenue Project who, in turn, had agreed that our museum would constitute the cultural component of their development. Somehow, in the supervisors' view, The Broad was an "elitist" institution grubbing for a public subsidy.

Nothing could have been further from the truth. The whole concept of The Broad was to take a world-class collection of the most important art of our time and make it accessible to as many people from as many walks of life as possible. Not only would our art be on view for anybody who walked through the door, but also The Broad Art Foundation would continue to serve as a lending library for other public art museums around the world. If there was an elitist assumption at work anywhere in that equation, it was the notion that working people are not inspired and enriched by the experience of thought-provoking art. The prospect of having to make that case was almost as tiresome as having our gift horse looked in the mouth. But I don't quit that easily.

I appraised the supervisors' incentives and realized that one of them was making a show of hardheaded stewardship for his constituents. I felt I had to bring him along because it was important to have unanimous support for such an important project. That's why we offered to pay $7.7 million for the site. I also reminded everyone that with the low admission price we planned to charge, the museum's proximity to public transportation, and the landscape improvements we would bring to Grand Avenue, The Broad would be far from elitist.

The reasonable thing to do in this situation would have been to choose a site in Santa Monica or Beverly Hills, where officials were eager to accommodate us for the sake of our collection's prestige. That, in fact, would have been the elitist thing to do. From the start, what we wanted was to make great contemporary art available to as many people as possible—and downtown L.A. was the best place to do that. As it turned out, getting the site required unreasonable persistence over several years, but I'm placing a big bet that future generations will be more than happy we stuck to it.

Even the Unreasonably Persistent Must Know When to Quit

Knowing when to quit is tricky, but if you are certain something is not going to work, you have to cut your losses immediately. Trying to avoid an inevitable loss isn't persistence—it's desperation. Sometimes you have to accept a loss so you can put all your energies, time, and money into the next project. As in negotiation, it's important to set a limit on what you're willing to expend—time, money, and pain—on reaching your goal. If you reach those limits, it's time to throw in the towel.

That's just as true when you're pursuing a good cause instead of profit. I learned this lesson when I tried to bring my favorite sport to my favorite city. Los Angeles hasn't had a professional football team since the Raiders left town in 1995, and it seemed to me that, for a host of reasons, a great American city ought to have a National Football League franchise. So in 1999 I teamed up with real estate developer Ed Roski Jr. in a bid to bring pro football back to L.A.

We put together a proposal, courted the league, and won the support of key city officials. The NFL was receptive to our $500 million bid, but at the eleventh hour, Houston came in with a $700 million offer, which included $260 million in public money to help build a new stadium. That was out of the question in Los Angeles, where popular opinion was set against any subsidies for pro sports. We had hit our limit and Houston simply was willing to go higher, so we lost. Frankly, I came away suspecting that the NFL had little incentive to award L.A. a franchise under any but the most outrageous conditions. After all, their national television ratings had soared even without a franchise in Los Angeles, and the revenues from their TV contracts are the key to the league's profitability. L.A. also serves a useful purpose as a bogey to frighten the cities that have teams: "If you don't build a new stadium, we're moving to Los Angeles."

My unsuccessful attempts to maintain local ownership of two other important civic institutions—the Dodgers baseball team and the *Los Angeles Times*—were equally frustrating, not least because the consequences for the city have been so unhappy.

The Dodgers had passed from the O'Malley family—whose patriarch, the legendary Walter, had moved the team from Brooklyn to Los Angeles in 1958—to Fox Sports, a unit of Rupert Murdoch's News Corporation, in 1998. The match wasn't a good one and Murdoch put the team back up for sale. After the company agreed to sell the Dodgers to Boston real estate developer Frank McCourt, who I learned was not a financially sound bidder, I made a late all-cash bid. I thought the team belonged in local hands. But Fox wanted to go ahead with the sale to McCourt. It was rumored that Major League Baseball Commissioner Bud Selig was concerned with the huge amounts Yankees owner George Steinbrenner and the Texas Rangers were paying to players, to the detriment of other teams in the league. Everyone assumed the commissioner would be reluctant to have another billionaire owner with deep pockets to sign the game's stars. Even though I made the best cash offer, Selig helped engineer the team's sale—on credit—to McCourt. As his messy divorce proceedings later revealed, McCourt and his wife essentially looted one of baseball's historic franchises to support the celebrity lifestyle they embraced when they moved to L.A.

The new owners forced the team into bankruptcy and had to sell. Looking back, I can see that the size and soundness of my bid just wasn't enough. If I had correctly projected the Dodgers's future potential revenues from television—which I underestimated—I might have sweetened my offer. But that still may not have done the trick.

Sometimes there are forces at play that are impermeable to either persuasion or logic. When you can see that's the case, get up from the table and move on to the next project.

The *Los Angeles Times* was, like the Dodgers, a civic icon, a symbol of L.A.'s status as a world-class city and a vital part of its political and cultural life. It, too, had passed out of local hands when the controlling Chandler family sold their Times Mirror Corporation to Chicago-based Tribune Company in 2000. It was an unhappy marriage from the start, and the Chandler interests on Tribune's board ultimately forced management to put Tribune up for sale too. Although I was only interested in the *Los Angeles Times*, I had to bid on the entire company, which also included the *Chicago Tribune* and seven other daily newspapers, 23 television stations, and the Chicago Cubs baseball team. I teamed with supermarket magnate and investor Ron Burkle to make a bid that would have brought ownership of the *Los Angeles Times* back home. Neither of us reckoned on Tribune's desire to keep the company headquartered in Chicago or on the creativity of prominent Chicago commercial real estate entrepreneur Sam Zell. He came up with a scheme to take the company private by creating an employee stock ownership program that theoretically made the employees co-owners. Despite the fact he put in a little more than $300 million of his own money, he also convinced a number of major banks to lend him the money to finance the deal.

There's leverage and there's folly. The Tribune-Zell deal was the latter because the company was insolvent virtually from the start, unable to service its debt as newspaper and broadcasting revenues from advertising fell across the board. Despite his promises, the only thing Zell could think to do was cut. The new owner essentially gutted the company's newspapers. Today, the *Los Angeles Times* is a shadow of its former self, and the damage to Southern California has been palpable.

Now, Tribune also is in bankruptcy—a lengthy and convoluted procedure that probably will be used as a cautionary case study by business schools for years to come. The only saving grace may come when the company emerges from Chapter 11 and the creditors put the *Los Angeles Times* up for sale, as they likely will do. This time around, the price should be better and the advantages of local ownership clear to all.

Sometimes you walk away so that you can have a second shot down the line to return. That's something to remember when your loss stings the most. There will be another day and, as long as you stay on the hunt, it will bring its own opportunities.

Chapter 16

IS THAT THE BEST YOU CAN DO? MOTIVATING PEOPLE BY CHALLENGING THEM

When I hired Bruce Karatz, who would go on to be the CEO of Kaufman and Broad, he was already a go-getter—a lawyer willing to give up the security of a law firm to work for a homebuilder.

For his first nonlegal assignment, I asked him to drive out to Riverside, about 90 minutes east of Los Angeles, to check out some land we were considering buying. Bruce was enthusiastic, went out there a few times, and wrote a report for me. I let a couple of days go by without responding, until Bruce came in and asked me what I thought.

"Is that the best you can do?" I asked.

Bruce looked a little worried. He said he would work on the report some more. When he brought it back, I asked him one more time: "Is that the best you can do?" He took it away, made some more revisions, and brought it back a third time. I asked him the same question again. By that time, Bruce was pretty sure he was about to be fired. He threw up his hands and said, "Yes, that's the best I can do."

"Good," I replied. "Now I'll read it."

Bruce felt a bit jerked around, but he was a good sport—and smart enough to see that I had managed to get his finest work. I never had to pull that stunt on him again because he knew that I expected his best effort. Years later, when executives at more than 100 companies were accused of backdating stock options, Bruce's high profile attracted the attention of federal prosecutors, who charged him with a raft of offenses. Ultimately, he was acquitted of any serious misconduct but convicted on three minor charges. At loose ends while awaiting sentencing—he ultimately received home confinement—Bruce threw himself into helping Los Angeles's most successful gang intervention program, Homeboy Industries. Founded by a Jesuit priest, the organization employs former gang members in a bakery, a café, and a variety of other occupations. When Bruce became involved, Homeboy was on the verge of collapse because demand for its services had grown while the recession had dried up its funding. Bruce applied his marketing genius and helped Homeboy generate new business and additional investors.

During the years we worked together directly, Bruce's performance always reminded me that your best motivator always is an unreasonably high goal.

High Expectations and Shared Challenges Create Loyalty

I like people who are self-motivated, as I am. But even the best athletes have coaches, and the brightest students need mentors.

I believe the best way to mentor is to challenge people and then to set an example by letting them see you in action. My former assistant Jay Wintrob, now president and CEO of SunAmerica Financial Group, calls me an "untraditional mentor" because from his earliest days on the job, I simply started handing him projects. I never sat him down and said, "This is the way I want you to approach this." I just sent him off and made sure he was comfortable coming to me with questions as they arose. To this day, Jay calls that my "go figure it out method" of leading. In fact, that was the line Alan Cranston used with me when he asked me to chair his Senate campaign.

I used that method many times throughout my career, particularly with Jana Greer, who you read about in Chapter 7. Jana, who is now president and CEO of AIG SunAmerica Retirement Markets, Inc., came to work for me when she was just 22. Not long after she joined, our vice president of corporate communications resigned. I called Jana to my office and asked, "So have you ever written an annual report?"

Jana later told me her first thought was, "I don't know that I've ever *read* an annual report." But all she said at the time was no. I informed her that she was about to write ours. She asked for examples and suggestions, which was the response I was hoping for. "You'll get it done," I told her. "I'm not worried at all." As it turned out, I was right. She got it done and she did an excellent job.

When you challenge people to dig deep and do more and better than even they imagined they could, it creates a particular bond. Certainly that was true for Jana, just as it was for Jay and for Bruce. To this day I share a fierce loyalty with each of them.

Nothing Motivates Like Achievement

I find that the most effective way to motivate people is to accomplish big things together. When you set the same unreasonable goals for your employees that you do for yourself, your expectation becomes a gesture of respect. That's what I hoped would happen when I gave our foundations' chief investment officer, Marc Schwartz, a particularly challenging task.

Facebook came to my attention in a personal way in 2010, when U.S. Secretary of Education Arne Duncan asked if I would meet with Facebook founder Mark Zuckerberg and brief him on our decade-long efforts to reform public education. Mark and his chief operating officer, Sheryl Sandberg, came to our home on a Saturday, and we spent several hours discussing the crisis facing America's public schools. Mark and Sheryl were impressive, smart, and driven. I appreciated that Mark was self-made and had all his own money tied up in his company. He had made all the right moves in starting the social media site and his thoughtful approach made me believe his batting average would remain high. Although I didn't understand all the nuances of social networking, I understood its potential to generate information and money for advertisers, especially for local businesses or start-ups. It was clearly a powerful model. I knew that if our foundations could secure a stake in his privately held company, we wouldn't have to wait 10 years to realize our investment's potential—probably more like one or two. I decided we needed to invest in Facebook.

I called Marc Schwartz into my office to tell him my idea. He had been working for me only a few months when I gave him the challenge: "Buy us a stake in Facebook. I don't care how you do it, but buy us a stake."

It would not be easy. Marc would have to find a fund or an employee who had shares in the company and needed liquidity. He would have to do a lot of research and talk to everyone he knew and somehow dig his way to a willing and credible seller.

I usually communicate with my investment team by phone, or they see me in my office. But after I laid out that goal, every time I saw Marc, and the times I called to check in, my first and sometimes only question was "Did you buy Facebook yet?" I could see the frustration on his face and hear it in his voice. Every time, he would say no and give me the latest roadblock he had hit and then start to say he didn't think it could be done as soon as I wanted it done. And every time, I replied, "Uh huh. Buy Facebook."

After several weeks of this, Marc hit pay dirt. His creativity and resourcefulness led us to a great find and a secure investment. My investment team likes to joke that I accept a no after the tenth no. Marc didn't quite hit 10, but we got close. Instead, because he was challenged to his limits, Marc found opportunity for us where even he was skeptical it could be found and certainly not in the timeframe I demanded.

We secured the bulk of our investment just before Goldman Sachs purchased a big chunk of Facebook, pushed its valuation way up, and launched a feeding frenzy, long before the company filed to go public. Had we waited, we never would have gotten our stake at the price we did, if at all.

WHAT'S BETTER THAN PRAISE—MONEY AND HIGHER EXPECTATIONS

I'm not effusive, even in moments of triumph, and I don't hand out compliments lightly. That makes my employees value them all the more when they receive them. It also means that I get the maximum impact from the positive feedback I give because the person hearing it knows I'm sincere. The best praise is specific, genuine, brief, and, ideally, followed by setting a new, more demanding goal. Entrusting people with greater responsibility and greater expectations is the highest form of praise.

A bonus tied to performance is even better than praise. Whether we're comfortable admitting it or not, material rewards are how we keep score in the business world. The best employees don't work solely for money, but nobody works without it. While I was running SunAmerica, if the company and our employees performed well, they would receive a bonus and additional stock options, which was pretty unorthodox at the time. Giving my team an immediate and concrete return on their efforts was better than a hundred flowery phrases. It also made them see the value in the challenges set for them.

FEAR IS NOT A MOTIVATOR—IT ONLY GETS YOU UNHAPPY EMPLOYEES AND POOR WORK

When it comes to motivating people, fear is as overrated as praise. I don't use it because it's disrespectful of employees. What's the point in demonstrating over and over that you're more powerful than they are?

I also don't believe in explosions of temper. For one thing, as you'll recall from our earlier examples, emotion clouds your judgment.

If your emotional outbursts simply provoke another emotional reaction—like fear—nobody benefits.

I don't casually tell people their jobs are at stake. I don't raise my voice, and I rarely curse. People know when I'm unhappy. But I don't express displeasure over failure if it's preceded by serious effort toward one of my unreasonable goals. This means my employees are never afraid to try and to fail. I still believe the same thing I said to Jay Wintrob when he first started: "Show me a person with an unblemished track record and I'll show you a person who has dramatically underachieved." There is a lot to be said for batting .600. If you're doing 10 things and only 4 are failing, that's pretty good.

Many of my senior employees, in fact, talk about my willingness to let them fail as long as they learn from the experience. Very early on in attorney Deborah Kanter's career with our foundation, I asked her to handle the purchase of some land from another major nonprofit institution. Her background was in tax and intellectual property, and the lawyers for the seller put something over on us. Although she had pushed beyond her expertise, Deborah felt she should have caught the sellers' maneuver. She came to me to report it, fully expecting to be fired. She told me precisely what had happened and that it was possibly too late to do anything about it.

I sat and thought for a minute. Then I said, "Well, I'm supposed to be the real estate expert. I should have caught it too. Let's see what we can do to mitigate any damage." We just moved on. In the end, it turned out that we were able to fix the initial problem. Deborah went on to tackle even more tasks outside her comfort zone. Most recently, she took on managing the construction of The Broad.

If you let your employees fail without punishment, you'll win their loyalty, their hardest effort, and their willingness to take risks with you. No one will resort to finger-pointing or cover-ups.

Think about the last time fear motivated you to do something well, to exceed your limits, or to really contribute. I'm guessing you won't recall a positive experience. Fear does not inspire loyalty, creativity, or genuine commitment. It's a waste of time.

WHETHER YOU SUCCEED OR FAIL, KEEP MOVING

If you don't reach your goal, or achieve only part of it, there's no shame. That's what's great about an unreasonable goal—even when you miss it, you'll probably get farther than you ever thought possible. If you fail, just figure out why, learn your lessons, and move on to the next thing.

And if you succeed, I recommend doing exactly the same thing: move on. Nothing breeds complacency quite like a string of successes. In that sense, success and failure can be equally dangerous—one can immobilize you with self-satisfaction and the other can paralyze you with fear. Think of them both as preparation for the next unreasonable challenge and use what you've learned to tackle it.

Chapter 17

COMPETITION

The late radio and television pioneer David Sarnoff once remarked, "Competition brings out the best in products and the worst in men."

The first part seems incontestable to me; the second is highly debatable.

I have always believed that competition pushes people, companies, and organizations to higher levels of achievement. I was always driven to be the best, to be first among our competitors. We competed in the arenas of stock price, market share, and reputation. But the other guy didn't set the higher bar. We set it ourselves.

My current careers in philanthropy and collecting contemporary art involve competition of a different sort. I'm competing against myself again—but it's not for profit. It's for the satisfaction that comes from making positive change and enriching more lives each year.

Just Because There's a Winner Doesn't Mean There's a Loser

Competition in business benefits the customer by stimulating better products and service and lower prices. The same holds for higher education, which has benefited from the strong rivalries between private and public institutions for faculty, students, and donors. In my hometown, for example, I doubt UCLA would be as exemplary a school as it is today were it not for the presence of USC and Caltech, among others.

But America's K–12 public schools have, until recently, been a monopoly. Most alternatives, such as private education or home schooling, are available only to families with resources. The rise of high-performing public charter schools has injected a much-needed dose of competition into our education system because they give parents a choice in where to send their children to school. Charter schools are public schools that operate under a granted charter that gives them greater flexibility in exchange for more accountability. If a charter school doesn't perform, it can be closed. The same doesn't hold for traditional public schools, many of which limp along with declining enrollment and abysmal student achievement. Charter schools have the flexibility to lengthen the school day, hold classes on Saturdays, pay their teachers more, and engage students through personalized learning. Because parents have the choice of sending their children to a traditional public school or a public charter school, the very existence of these schools creates competition. And when state and local funding go to whatever school a student attends, it's in a school's best interest to keep its students and attract new ones. Some of our highest performing charter grantees even use the term *coopetition* to describe how they cooperate with one another and share best practices. While each strives to produce the highest student achievement gains, they root for one another because they know the true winners are the students.

It's wrong to think that competition automatically means there are winners and losers. Our foundations encourage fair competition, with no losers, through initiatives like our $1 million Broad Prize for Urban Education. We award it annually to the urban public school districts that show the greatest improvement in student achievement while narrowing gaps among poor and minority children. None of the finalists for the prize loses. We award college scholarships to students in the winning school district and to students in the finalist districts. Districts have even set the goal of winning The Broad Prize in their strategic plan, and we're happy to provide an incentive that encourages them to boost the academic progress of their students. Because of the success of The Broad Prize, we recently launched a $250,000 Broad Prize for Public Charter Schools, which goes to the charter management organization that annually demonstrates the most outstanding student gains and that helps students of all backgrounds advance.

ARCHITECTURE—THE PUREST FORM OF COMPETITION

Competition exists, to a certain degree, in every area—business, families, education, philanthropy. But there is one area where competition is at its purest: architecture.

Architectural competitions have become fairly common for major private and public projects. I have been fortunate enough to participate in several significant ones—most recently for The Broad.

For most projects, you start with a site and a purpose in mind for a building. Then you examine the field and come up with a list of five or six architects to submit their best designs for realizing your vision. They often create elaborate three-dimensional models and present them to a jury that selects the winner. The results almost always are better—often strikingly so—than if you had simply chosen an architect for the commission. (I think the one world-class architect whose work is not improved by traditional industry competition is Frank Gehry. That's because he's always locked in competition with himself.)

THE UNEXPECTED PLUSES OF ARCHITECTURE COMPETITIONS

It makes perfect sense that a competition—not to mention all the media attention and expert scrutiny that come with it—would make architects do their best work. But one thing I find fascinating about these competitions is that they often push the jurors and patrons as hard as they do the architects. Like spectators witnessing any competition, jurors examining architecture designs are often moved to reconsider their personal limits and set their ambitions a little higher.

Take, for example, Zaha Hadid's design for The Broad Art Museum at my alma mater, Michigan State University. We brought in a nationally known architecture and design writer, Joseph Giovannini, to oversee the competition. An initial field of 30 firms was reduced to 10 semifinalists. Then five were invited to submit final designs. At the start of the process, the university's president, Lou Anna Simon, had given us all a strong caution that she thought the final building had to respect the traditional brick-and-ivy architecture of the campus. But when the final designs came in, President Simon was the one pushing for the most extreme entry—Hadid's building, an intensely sculptural series of low-to-the-ground, interconnected metal and glass trapezoids. Given where President Simon started, I found her transition instructive about the power of observing competitions. Even if you're not in the game, you're driven to expand your mind.

Another competition I was involved in managed to transform not just the jurors but also the whole idea of how to construct an affordable public building in California. The state wanted to build a new California Department of Transportation (Caltrans) headquarters in downtown Los Angeles's civic center. Then Governor Gray Davis told me he wanted it to be an important piece of architecture but within a strict budget. I convinced him to scrap the traditional request for proposals process and instead undertake an architectural competition. He asked me to spearhead the selection, so I brought in the head of the Art Center College of Design, Richard Koshalek. With both Davis's desire and the budget in mind, we came up with a new way to run the competition. We asked each architect to team up with a developer and a contractor. Together, they would submit not only a design but also a plan to construct it at a fixed price.

The winner was Thom Mayne of Morphosis, who produced an extraordinary design, but he ultimately said he couldn't bring it in on budget. At the last minute, I had to intervene to help cut costs. I convinced Caltrans they would have to accept tandem parking in the garage, told the contractor his contingency fee was too large, and then broke the news to Thom Mayne that he just wasn't going to get everything he wanted in the design. After all sorts of finagling, we still were $2 million short, so Edye and I stepped in to cover the shortfall. They named the building's plaza after us. The best thing, though, was that the civic center got a striking piece of architecture.

Sometimes a competition produces a winner but no building. That was the case with the contest we conducted for the redesign of the Los Angeles County Museum of Art (LACMA) campus.

I was on the LACMA board at the time, and in my typical fashion, set about putting together an architecture competition as fast as possible. To kick things off, I borrowed a jet from Hank Greenberg of AIG so that I could take museum officials to meet the architects we were considering. We left from the Van Nuys airport at 6:30 AM and arrived in Europe at 12:30 AM the next morning. We visited architects in five cities—London, Paris, Berlin, Basel, and Rotterdam—over four days. (Then LACMA Director Andrea Rich called it the Bataan Death March.) The architect I wanted the most was Renzo Piano. He had designed the Beyeler Foundation, an art museum in Switzerland, among several other great buildings known for their smart use of light. But Renzo informed us that he doesn't participate in competitions. With him out of the running, we got proposals from five other architects and finally selected Rem Koolhaas.

Koolhaas's proposal was completely different from everyone else's. He also gave a standout in-person presentation. He managed to persuade us that he could tear down everything and rebuild the museum within a huge, tentlike structure that would stand on stilts, leaving a big public space underneath. He said this could be done in stages, but after five or six months and a lot of meetings, we discovered that wasn't possible. At the very least, the entire museum would have to be shut down for two or three years, which was out of the question. We suddenly realized why, brilliant architect though he is, a lot of Koolhaas's buildings never get built.

That was disappointing because I thought his design was fascinating, but it did open the door for us to add a new contemporary art museum to LACMA. Edye and I pledged $50 million toward the construction of The Broad Contemporary Art Museum (BCAM) and added another $10 million for art acquisition. LACMA had undertaken a competition whose winner produced a design that couldn't be built. But that failure freed us to recruit the architect who had no interest in competing but who I knew would design a wonderfully functional building.

Edye and I flew to Paris to convince Renzo Piano to do the design. I told him it would be a great commission because we knew what we wanted, we had the money, and he wouldn't have to deal with anyone but Andrea Rich and me.

As I expected, Renzo was not an easy sell. First he said he had too much work. Then he said he would think about it while he went sailing over the weekend. I asked him where he would be the next Monday. He said London. I said I'd meet him there. It was in London that we convinced him to come to Los Angeles and take a look at the site.

Renzo gave us another no. He said he wasn't interested unless he could execute a more sweeping master plan. With that, he went back home. I flew after him for one last ask—as I said, I don't take no for an answer the first few times. This time we met in his office in Genoa. It sits on a hilltop overlooking the Mediterranean, accessible only by a little rail car that runs up the steep incline. I prevailed on Renzo to commit to BCAM, and he finally agreed.

After all that time-consuming back-and-forth, Renzo designed a building that is a marvel of efficiency. I like to say that the best buildings result when there is a strong client and a strong architect. One of my unreasonable demands was to maximize the gallery space. I questioned every convention of a museum: Did the stairs need to be inside the building? Could the electrical and lighting systems be designed another way? Did we really need multiple bathrooms? Clearly, I lost on that last point. In the end, Renzo designed BCAM so that 90 percent of the building is devoted to gallery space.

CONCEPT OVER COST

As an architectural patron and client, I will often sacrifice cost for concept, something I would generally not do in business.

After serving on architectural competitions for years, I recently had the opportunity to run our own competition for The Broad. And for someone who likes to control the process, this was my chance to do things my way. What I found, though, was that even when you have oversight and ultimate accountability for every aspect of a project, it's not without a fair share of frustrations.

When Edye and I decided to build a museum to house our personal and foundation art collections, we wanted an architecturally significant building. When we selected the site on Grand Avenue, we knew our museum couldn't clash with neighboring Walt Disney Concert Hall, but it couldn't fade into the background either. The building had to serve two functions: as a public museum and as the headquarters for The Broad Art Foundation's lending library. It would mean that in addition to expansive galleries, the building had to have storage space for artworks when they weren't on public view in our museum or elsewhere. And the site had its own restrictions. It was a full city block—a nearly perfect square parcel—and had a three-story height limit. What we would ask of architects was, essentially, to build a box. Architects aren't often thrilled by restrictions.

We invited six internationally renowned architects to compete, convened a jury of architecture scholars and museum directors, and finally selected the design of Diller Scofidio + Renfro, the New York team that had designed and renovated the expansion of Lincoln Center, the Institute of Contemporary Art on Boston Harbor, and the innovative High Line park in lower Manhattan. Architect Elizabeth Diller came up with a unique concept for combining public exhibition space with storage. Dubbed "the vault and the veil," Liz's proposal was to make the storage space the literal core of the building. The heavy opaque mass of the second floor "vault" would be in constant view, hovering midway in the building, while its carved underside shaped the lobby and its top surface provided the floor of the exhibition space. The "veil," then, would wrap the entire building with a cellular structure made of concrete and provide diffused natural daylight.

We picked the design because it accomplished all of our objectives, even though it was estimated to cost $10 million more than the other designs.

The unreasonable nature of art and architecture is that it usually fails to conform to convention. We found that to be particularly true when it came time to build The Broad. We fell in love with the design because it was truly unique and had not been done before. That carries with it a risk and, in our case, a much larger price tag. We had been assured that a fabricator in Southern California could build the concrete veil, but the costs kept escalating. We finally found a fabricator in Germany who could use a different material but keep the integrity of the design. Alterations and compromises are often required to bring a great concept to reality.

The museum is under construction and expected to open in early 2014. Although I scour the budget and question every expense, I know that, whatever the cost, we will get exactly what we wanted: A public contemporary art museum in the heart of the city's cultural center and an iconic piece of architecture that could have resulted only from pure competition.

Chapter 18

IT'S BETTER TO BE RESPECTED THAN LOVED

I'm not the most popular person in Los Angeles.

When you're unreasonable, even for a good cause, you inevitably rub people the wrong way. People also tend to mistake focus for brusqueness. When you really believe that the shortest distance between two points is a straight line, it's hard to zigzag for the sort of small talk or conventional gestures that soothe egos. As you'll recall from earlier chapters, I've always thought that was a waste of time. I'm never uninterested in other people's ideas or contributions, but frankly I am relatively indifferent to their opinion of me.

Not caring what people think of you is a difficult quality to cultivate, but if you do, there is much you can accomplish. You just have to understand that being respected is more important than being loved. Respect is also easier to obtain. You only have to hold yourself to high standards, treat people fairly, and get things done.

And trust me, nothing patches over bruised egos and imagined slights like success. When your unreasonable focus accomplishes something, suddenly everyone is glad to be around you and eager for a share of the credit. Be as generous with credit as you are tight-fisted with your time. It doesn't cost you anything and leaves people eager for future collaborations.

DISAGREEMENT IS HEALTHY—LEARN HOW TO
DISTINGUISH IT FROM DISSENT

Whether you're running a business or leading a community initiative, it's important that you and your employees or collaborators have the same goal. There will, and there should be, many different ways to get there. Disagreeing over the "how" is the only way to find the right path. You should encourage disagreement when it's expressed in respectful, commonsense debate and doesn't become personal or heated. Once you've heard everyone out and reached a logical decision on the correct way to go, though, you can't have dissent.

Debate always has to end, and someone has to decide a way forward. Very often that someone has been me, and it's the main reason why I ruffle feathers. But if you're in charge, that someone is you, whatever others may think of you and your conclusions.

GOOD PRINCIPLES ARE PORTABLE—STICK TO THEM

Believe it or not, I used to ruffle more feathers than I do now.

Earlier in my career, I had an even greater distaste for the conventions of social glad-handing and making nice than I do now. I was focused on the mission, and that was that. I simply assumed people would appreciate me for the results I got, and because that was the standard by which I judged myself, I was content to let them do the same.

In the business world, this was largely acceptable. Although there are entrepreneurs who succeed by charm, the rest of us do it by hard work, innovation, and sticking to the mission we've set for ourselves. Steve Jobs, the phenomenally creative late CEO of Apple, was famous for his caustic dismissal of ideas that didn't measure up in his eyes. Look, however, at his record of success. William Randolph Hearst, who built one of America's great publishing empires, famously told the reporters in his first newspaper's city room not to remove their hats when at their desks. That way they wouldn't have to stop to retrieve them if they were fired. I'm neither as imperious as Jobs nor as cavalier about other people's fates as Hearst, but focus on a mission and a keen attention to time and the bottom line always have defined my relations with other people.

If that has made me less than loved, I simply point to my business and philanthropic accomplishments and keep on moving.

When I began to participate on the boards of nonprofits, where the rules were a little different, it's fair to say I rubbed a lot of people the wrong way. My first board appointment was to Pitzer College, which I joined in 1970. Not long after, my goal was to help make the place financially sound. The school was only 7 years old, but the faculty and my fellow board members behaved as if they were stewards of a long-established institution with an overflowing endowment. Obviously, we were no stewards, and the endowment was nowhere near overflowing.

The first thing I wanted to do was to instill some financial discipline from top to bottom. My point seemed, to me anyway, perfectly unobjectionable. I argued that a college couldn't keep hiking tuition to pay for higher salaries. It had to raise funds from other sources, not just from students, who were already paying an arm and a leg. And it was hard to raise new money when people were uncertain about how wisely the college was spending what it had. But instead of agreeing, everyone was annoyed with me, from my colleagues on the board to the college president to the faculty. People balked at my blunt criticism. But I didn't back down, and over time Pitzer achieved sounder financial footing.

As much as my candor may have initially angered those with a stake in the school's status quo, I eventually was named chairman of the board for my work. That was an expression of respect for what I had been able to do for a terrific college. I'll take that over first place in a popularity contest any day. If you stop and think about it, I'll bet you would too.

LET GO OF POWER BEFORE YOU LET GO OF PRINCIPLES

My candor also ruffled feathers back in the 1980s on the board of MOCA, which I chaired in the early years after the museum was founded. My fellow board members felt I was autocratic because I wanted our meetings to have an agenda and to start and end on time. I also wanted to keep tabs on our budget and endowment, and I wanted people to give me clear and timely information to help do that. I didn't think it was a lot to ask, but apparently some of my colleagues did.

Unfortunately, the boards of art institutions tend to be populated with well-meaning supporters of the arts who often lack any business background or appetite for imposing appropriate discipline. My style didn't seem like a good fit for the board. When it became clear that our clashing methods were getting in the way of our shared goal, I bowed out.

Even so, I kept up my support for MOCA and my interest in a world-class contemporary art institution for our city. I simply decided that the best way for me to contribute to that goal was from a different position than head of the board. People came and went from that board, but the culture of lax oversight deepened until 2008, when wastefulness and inattention brought the museum to the brink of insolvency.

Sometimes, circumstances dictate that you get up and walk away, but they should never compel you to wholly abandon something in which you believe. That's why Edye and I stepped in with an offer to provide a $30 million challenge grant, an approach a lot of philanthropies use to leverage their funds. We promised $15 million to match whatever MOCA could raise from other sources to replenish the endowment and another $3 million a year for five years to support major exhibitions. The grants came with the condition that the museum would agree to put itself on a sustainable footing and not to sell any of its art to meet expenses. Ultimately, our offer was accepted and MOCA—with its collection intact—remains one of the city's great cultural assets.

Don't Become Ensnared by Egos—Not Even Your Own

If you're as unreasonable as I am, you have to try to factor into the equation how people will react to your style. I learned that the hard way while fund-raising for the Walt Disney Concert Hall.

As I described earlier, I worked with Andrea Van de Kamp and Dick Riordan to get fund-raising back on track. Once the ball was rolling, I knew we had to move fast. The price of materials was due to spike, and we had promised all our donors that we would be done building within a few years.

But people had begun to grumble that the building's architect, Frank Gehry, had produced a design that just was too complicated and expensive to build. Frank is a Pritzker Prize winner and one of inter-national architecture's true superstars. The museum he designed for the Guggenheim in Bilbao, Spain, was a global sensation and put the city on the world's cultural map. It was pretty clear, though, that con-structing the concert hall he had designed for Los Angeles *was* going to be expensive and hellishly complex.

I had some experience with Frank, and it was not an entirely happy history. Edye and I had commissioned him to design our home in Los Angeles. Frank's office didn't do construction documents at the time he was designing our house. After two years and seven designs—all of which I approved—I pushed Frank to finish. We hired the firm he recommended to do the construction documents, but he just wasn't happy with my urging him to hurry, and we parted ways.

We had a similar situation with Disney Hall. Frank's office had hired another firm, Dworsky Architecture, to do the construction documents, but after several million dollars was spent on the documents, Frank decided they were not usable. Dick and Andrea both agreed with me that, because Frank was done with his design, we should go ahead and hire someone else to put together the construction documents—and fast. But then Frank claimed only he could do construction documents. I didn't back down and insisted that we needed to bring someone else in to get us moving. That's when Frank submitted his resignation.

I have to say I was surprised. The press rushed to write stories that I had gotten into "another fight" with Frank. But within a week of his resignation, we all met and agreed that no one wanted Frank off the project. We reaffirmed that our goal was to get a Gehry-designed hall built on time. We agreed to disagree about whether "on time" would happen if Frank continued working on the project.

In this instance, I wasn't the decision maker. Diane Disney Miller stepped in to make sure Frank stayed on and that his fees would be covered. I was not about to fight with the woman whose family's generosity made the hall possible in the first place. I wasn't going to let my ego get in the way of realizing a magnificent new asset for the city. You have to know when you're the one whose feathers are ruffling and when not to insist you're right just for the sake of winning.

From then on, I stayed focused on fund-raising, and Frank stuck to the project. The timeline, as I had suspected, stretched out quite a lot. But keeping Diane and Frank on board and building the hall was the most important thing. When the hall was finished, Frank gave a celebratory dinner on the stage to thank Dick, Andrea, and me. Today Disney Hall is Los Angeles's brightest cultural jewel—admired everywhere as a superb-sounding concert hall and a brilliantly imagined building.

A few years later, I urged the Related Companies, which was developing the Grand Avenue Project, to hire Frank to design the first phase. Even though Frank and I don't always see eye to eye, I have a tremendous amount of respect for his talent, and he has been generous with his advice and wise counsel on our new museum and many other projects. Today, I consider Frank a good friend.

IF YOU'RE IN THE WAY, MOVE

From earlier chapters, you know something of my vision for turning downtown Los Angeles's Grand Avenue into the central civic and cultural district of the region.

As part of that vision, I pushed for an architecturally significant design for the school district's new Central Los Angeles High School

No. 9. Despite the bureaucratic label, the school is a public arts campus situated at the northernmost end of Grand Avenue. It's hard to imagine a better symbolic entry point to a grand boulevard alive with arts and culture than a free public school dedicated to educating young people of every background in the visual and performing arts.

Not long after Disney Hall opened, I had visited LaGuardia High School in New York City, the arts school depicted in the movie *Fame*. I was impressed by the activity within those halls—ballet, sculpture, painting, music—and the determination of the students to master their disciplines. I came to believe that Los Angeles, a city with so many working artists and a visual and performing arts mecca, needed a similar state-of-the-art school for its talented students, particularly those from working- and middle-class families.

I encouraged the school board to drop its plan for an ordinary public school at the site in favor of something that—although more expensive because of its world-class design and its arts curriculum—would capture the spirit, excitement, and talent surging through our city. I wanted a building that would inspire students before they ever walked through its doors. Eventually, the school board came around to the idea. They held an architectural competition, and the jury selected a design by Viennese architect Wolf Prix. The final design required some compromise, but it would still be a magnificent building that would hold its own across the freeway from Spanish architect José Rafael Moneo's monumental Roman Catholic Cathedral of Our Lady of the Angels.

Once building started, though, I took some stiff hits in the local press. Some district officials believed I was exerting undue influence over the new school. You would be surprised how derisive the word *billionaire* can sound when thrown with the right spin. But I brushed it off and stuck to my idea: That the district needed a great flagship school for the arts, not just another run-of-the-mill campus for our students.

Then I was criticized for wanting the school to draw student talent from across the city, rather than solely from among nearby residents. We ended up compromising on that point, devoting most of the seats to local students until overcrowding in neighborhood schools eased. I got some heat for the price of the school, although much of the cost overrun came from clearing the site, the failure to lock in materials prices at a low rate, and the district's mismanagement. (Somehow they miscalculated the square footage of the building.)

For a while, I tried to do what I did at MOCA and Disney Hall—compromise and revise my role. To support the school and its fund-raising, I created a committee that included arts giants such as Plácido Domingo, Quincy Jones, and Tony Bennett. I promised to donate up to $5 million through our foundation—as long as the school showed headway in developing a curriculum, appointed an executive director for fund-raising, and recruited a talented principal. But nothing happened. I even tried to convince the mayor to make it a charter school. That didn't work either.

With criticism continuing at a high pitch, I knew I could no longer be an effective advocate for the school. I bowed out—something I rarely do. I don't recommend it, unless you're becoming an obstacle to the very cause you want to support.

The school district never was able to recruit a well-regarded arts principal. Several of the country's leading arts educators came to town, considered the position, and then said they wanted no part of a stifling school district bureaucracy and rigid collective bargaining agreement.

Nothing Wins People Over Like Success

The overall Grand Avenue Project, although slowed because of the poor economy, is still moving along. The high school has been built and casts a striking profile at the street's northern end. Thanks to my convincing the Grand Avenue Project developer, Related Companies, to pay the city a $50 million down payment—which you'll recall from an earlier chapter—a civic park is nearly complete, linking City Hall and the Music Center. And we're building The Broad across the street from Disney Hall and MOCA.

Although it's all taken longer than I wanted—but then, nearly everything does—I'm confident that the redevelopment of Grand Avenue will get done. People want to live downtown again. Population in the district keeps growing. Crowds flock to L.A. Live, the sports and entertainment complex just off Grand Avenue's southern end. New businesses and restaurants are opening across the area. Millions of people who never set foot in downtown now consider it a destination—for sports, music, the visual arts, a great dinner, and spiritual reflection. Nobody thought it could be done. But it happened, thanks to the effort of a lot of persistent people and despite a lot of criticism.

Ruffled feathers should never get in the way of anything you really believe in and want to do. If you're starting a business or, frankly, doing anything that flies in the face of conventional wisdom, you're going to get some push back and sometimes even abuse. But if you stay the course, you'll be surprised at how quickly success wins people over, no matter what they think of you.

Chapter 19

GIVING BACK

My parents were hardworking but not wealthy people. My father painted houses until he saved up enough to open his own five-and-dime. My mother was a seamstress and later worked in the store and kept my dad's books.

Obviously, they didn't have money to give away, but they were generous with what they did have to spare—time and passion. My father spent many of his off-hours helping out at the Workmen's Circle, a nationwide Jewish social, political, and charitable organization whose left-wing politics he shared. Most of my parents' friends also were involved in the circle, which, as the name suggests, was concerned with labor issues and with enriching the lives of working people. The Workmen's Circle launched a network of Yiddish schools for children, ran housing cooperatives in our Bronx neighborhood, and pooled funds for everything from strike benefits to burials.

My parents also helped support my mother's brother, Joseph, who was one of the few family members to stay behind in Europe. He went to a university in Berlin, but when it came time to decide whether to go to America or stay in Western Europe—where it was becoming difficult for Jews to live in peace—Joseph chose a third option. Despite the precariousness of his own situation, Joseph worked to establish a school for Jewish children in British Palestine. The tradition of scholarship was deeply rooted among Lithuanian Jews. Among the graduates of the school my uncle helped found in Palestine is the two-time prime minister and current Israeli President Shimon

Peres. My uncle ended up being a character in Leon Uris's best-selling chronicle of the birth of Israel, *Exodus.*

I still remember my Uncle Joseph's visit to the Bronx when I was a boy. I recall his kind face and his hunchback. He was humble, an extraordinary example of a man devoted to giving without expecting anything in return. Uncle Joseph taught me you don't have to be rich to give—and that what you give can change the world.

My strongest example of that philosophy, though, was my mother, who named me for her grandfather Eliezer. My mom and I had a great deal in common. We were both instinctive savers rather than spenders, and we shared an intellectual bent. My mother also had an appetite for long hours and hard work that I inherited. She stayed late at the store and, when my father was out socializing, she cooked for me and did his accounts. Neither of us was as outgoing as he was. My mother was quiet but easy to talk to. Despite her prosperous upbringing, she was gifted with a needle. If she simply saw someone with an expensive dress and coat, she could make patterns and sew perfect replicas for her sisters. She gave, with an incredible selflessness, all she had to her family. And when my mother got sick in her later years, she came to live with us at Edye's insistence.

I chose the epitaphs for my parents' headstones. On my mother's I had engraved, "Nobody Had a Better Mother," and on my father's, "He Loved Life."

I'm still trying to live by their examples.

Everyone Can Be a Philanthropist—Not Just the Rich

The words *philanthropy* and *charity* once meant simply the love of humanity, the former from the Greek and the latter from Latin. Somewhere along the way, the meaning of each term narrowed. Charity became almost pejorative—a handout, a kind of help that was unwanted and did more for the giver than the recipient. Philanthropy, meanwhile, came to be considered the province of rich people.

Today, philanthropy has become a sophisticated undertaking by successful professionals aided by a staff. This new notion of philanthropy has, without a doubt, improved giving for the better. Creating a cadre of professional managers and bringing the best practices of the business world to bear makes giving well-researched, well-reasoned, well-executed, and accountable at every step of the way. Philanthropy aims to make the world a more peaceful, prosperous, wiser, healthier, and more livable place. Philanthropy may be conceived as an exercise of the heart, but those are goals worthy of our head's best efforts. That's not to say that check-writing charity doesn't have its place. What counts is that you give. For me, though, hands-on philanthropy is the more meaningful way to give back.

And philanthropy isn't just a pursuit for the wealthy. My parents' example demonstrates just how wrong that is. Philanthropy is about involvement. Pick your issue, work at it, and do your best to make things happen. Even if you're not wealthy, you have time, expertise, skills, and other resources you may not even have realized can be used to serve others.

Don't Just Give It Away—Look for the Place to Make a Difference

If you want to be actively involved in a philanthropic pursuit, don't check your critical and intellectual faculties at the door of any cause— no matter how worthy it appears. It's surprising how many people still hand away their money and time without thinking about whether they're doing the most good or achieving the greatest change with their efforts. Too often donations are based only on sudden, impulsive pangs of the heart, which, although understandable and admirable, may fall short of producing the results the donor wants.

That's why it's crucial that you apply an appropriate set of metrics to your giving. Make sure in advance that you have some way to measure the impact of your investment. If you're in a position to be generous enough to make grants, it can only help to know from the start what results you and your grantee want to achieve. However unreasonable it may seem, there's nothing hard-hearted or domineering about holding those to whom you give accountable. When our foundations invest in education reform, for example, we want to see many more students, of all income and ethnic backgrounds, making dramatic academic improvements. In scientific and medical research, we look for proof that scientists are getting closer to curing diseases and improving human lives around the world. We track our progress by how many groundbreaking journal articles, published papers, clinical trials, and patents our grantees generate. When we make grants to arts organizations, we expect increases in their audiences and museum traffic.

Whether you're making a foundation grant or deciding to which organization you want to donate your time, talent, and money, you should have an idea of what your beneficiary's success will look like. The goal can be distant, but there should be a clear one.

START GIVING NOW—AND IT DOESN'T HAVE TO BE MONEY

Edye and I were early signatories to the Giving Pledge, which was conceived by Bill and Melinda Gates and Warren Buffett. A lot of us were dubbed pretty unreasonable by our peers because by signing we promised to donate the bulk of our net worth to philanthropic efforts during or after our lifetimes.

I understand it's a little harder to decide how much to give when you have limited dollars to work with. Some people, like the ethicist Peter Singer, will tell you to give away half your money. It's an admirable goal but one I would say is impossibly unreasonable for most people, out of reach when you have to worry about providing for your children, holding on to your home, having enough money for retirement, or being able to cover your health costs. Some religious faiths suggest giving 10 percent of your annual income, which I believe is a sound and generous goal that many people can achieve, yet too few do. Dozens of companies in Minneapolis, Minnesota, following Target's lead, give 5 percent of their pretax net income, another worthy effort.

If you run a business and you aren't yet doing some type of philanthropy, there's no reason to wait. In the past, only the biggest corporations pursued philanthropy. Today, consumers and corporate culture demand that all profitable companies give something back. Some business models factor in philanthropy, a smart way to create change and win loyal customers. Take TOMS, the Santa Monica, California–based, for-profit shoe company. For each shoe a customer buys, the company donates a pair to a child in need. TOMS founder Blake Mycoskie created the company based on that principle.

Think about how you can use your business's expertise and competitive advantage to make a difference. Apply your business's special skills—whether it's Web design or baking—to doing good. Give your employees some time to pursue volunteer work. Chances are, they will take more pride in their work for you and your organization.

And, as always, lead by example. Too many entrepreneurs think they will get around to giving back when they have more spare time— something likely to remain in short supply. If you find yourself in that position, follow Warren Buffett's example. You don't have to re-create the wheel by starting your own foundation. Give to somebody else's, as Buffett did to the Gates Foundation. But if you want to donate a portion of your wealth to someone else's foundation, make sure you agree with the causes they support and their approach to philanthropy.

When you give, don't be afraid to talk about it. It can only help bring a good cause to other people's attention. Think back to the chapter on leverage, because its lessons also apply to philanthropy. Speaking publicly about the causes you've embraced is important because many nonprofit organizations depend on such exposure to get attention and do more good. My desire to leave an admirable legacy, and to honor my parents, is only part of the reason I've had our family's name inscribed on the buildings we fund. I've always thought seeing our name there—and knowing all the good work that goes on inside—would challenge others to give too.

Be a Philanthropic Game Changer—Start Local and Think Like an Entrepreneur

At The Broad Foundations, we give where we believe we can be game changers. Edye and I had the good fortune to be advised by our board member Larry Summers, the former Harvard president, U.S. Treasury secretary, and economic advisor to President Barack Obama. He helped us define our three criteria for making a philanthropic investment:

1. Will it make a difference in 20 years?
2. Would it happen anyway without our support?
3. Do we have the right people to make it happen?

Those three tests have helped set a course for our philanthropic investments. The best illustration is the Broad Institute in Cambridge.

We added to our work in education reform and the arts and decided to invest in the field of scientific and medical research, because we saw opportunities in genomics and stem cell research that passed our three tests.

In the case of The Broad Institute, we didn't know whether scientists from different fields would be willing to get out of their separate, far-flung labs to work together. We also weren't sure whether a partnership between Harvard and MIT would work, because it never had been attempted. And we had a lot of money riding on the answers.

The institute has been a great bet. And although we do take big risks in philanthropy, I am a bit more cautious than I was in business. The money we're working with—all of it earmarked to do good and all of it growing through investments—is precious. In a sense, instead of shareholders, we work for future generations who stand to benefit from the change we can create. That's a constituency we can't afford to disappoint.

Chapter 20

EDUCATION: NEVER LET A CRISIS GO TO WASTE

For one difficult year, I was an assistant professor at the Detroit Institute of Technology. It was a year after I graduated from MSU and started my fledgling accounting practice. I taught all the unglamorous night courses that no one else wanted, such as drugstore accounting. I scoured lesson plans, textbooks, and teachers' guides and tried as hard as I could to keep the attention of my 40 students each evening. A lot of them were older than I was, worked two or more jobs, or had just come back from fighting in Korea. Public speaking made me nervous back then, and some of my students fell asleep on me. I can't say I blame them. It was incredibly challenging work that left me with a lifelong respect for teachers.

Now, nearly 60 years later, that early experience has become all the more important because of our philanthropic work in education. One of our family's greatest priorities is to transform urban school districts by putting in place the leadership, innovations, policies, and institutions that enable students and teachers to succeed.

Given the scale of the problem, working to fix public education is the most unreasonable mission I've ever taken on.

THE WORLD IS MOVING FORWARD, BUT AMERICAN EDUCATION IS STAGNANT

I am old enough to remember when America's K–12 public schools were the best in the world. I am a proud graduate of them, and I credit

139

much of my success to what I learned in Detroit Public Schools and at Michigan State University. When I was in high school, not long after World War II, the United States had the top graduation rate. Since then, we have dropped behind 20 other industrialized nations. In less time than you just spent reading the last few paragraphs, another American student has dropped out of school. American students today rank 31st in the world in mathematics and 23rd in science. If the academic rankings of our most precious resource—our young people— were the rankings of our Olympic athletes, it would be a source of major national embarrassment.

The most shameful part of the picture—the one that, by my count, is the civil rights issue of our time—is the dramatically lower graduation rates for poor and minority students. These students are far less likely to have access to the best teachers.

By any measure, America's schools are in the grip of a profound crisis.

Frankly, I'm not sure how far I would get if I attended public school today. It's not just that public schools aren't producing the results we want—it's that we're not giving them what they need to help students achieve at high levels. K–12 education in the United States is deeply antiquated. Most schools still have a three-month summer vacation, a practice that dates back to our agrarian past, when most Americans lived on farms and children were required to help tend and harvest crops. Most classrooms are still physically set up the way they were then, with a teacher facing rows of students. Children of many different backgrounds and learning styles are expected to learn the same lesson taught in the same way. School district policies and practices have not kept pace with student and teacher needs.

Although classrooms have stayed largely the same on the inside, the world around them has changed radically. The sheer pace of economic and societal forces as a result of the digital revolution, for example, far exceeds the capacity of our schools, as they are currently structured, to keep up. How absurd that our students tuck their cell phones, BlackBerrys, iPads, and iPods into their backpacks when they enter a classroom and pull out a tattered textbook. Technological advances, such as iPads and iPhones, have personalized every arena of our lives, but very little has been done to harness the same power to personalize learning for students with different needs.

Classrooms in China, India, Japan, and South Korea, meanwhile, have advanced by leaps and bounds. They have elevated the teaching profession, insisted on longer school days and years, promoted education as a key value, created national ministries empowered to set priorities and standards, and built school cultures designed to help teachers uphold these high standards. They do all of this with far less money than the United States spends on education. In the past few decades, American taxpayer spending in real dollars has more than doubled with no associated increase in student achievement. Efforts to spend more money may be well intentioned, but money alone won't fix our schools.

The American middle class, once bolstered by well-paying jobs in the manufacturing and construction sectors that didn't require a higher education, now runs on service and technology sector jobs that require a significantly greater level of educational attainment. But too few young people are making it to college. Even when they do, the monumental cost of higher education and their unfortunate lack of sound K–12 preparation make the university track not just difficult, but also, in the eyes of an increasing number, undesirable. Without a sound education, these young people face higher rates of poverty, unemployment, and crime. Lifetime income, taxes, productivity, and health indicators all decline.

These are the kind of problems—lack of opportunity now and cynicism about the future—that contribute toward frustrations behind movements like Occupy Wall Street. They are right. We must do better.

IF THERE'S A CRISIS, GET INVOLVED AND MAKE A CHANGE

In the 1970s I began my philanthropic career by serving on the boards of Pitzer College and the California State University system. Higher education is where Edye and I made our first eight-figure gifts back in 1991: $10 million for Pitzer to add buildings on campus, the first such expansion since the college's founding, and $20 million to my alma mater, Michigan State University, to create a graduate school of management and a full-time Master of Business Administration program.

Through these roles, I quickly learned that the larger systemic issues in education were not, in fact, within higher education, but rather began at the primary and secondary levels. That's why students weren't making it to college or doing as well as they could.

When we started to invest more deeply in education philanthropy after merging SunAmerica with AIG, infusing our foundation with more than $1 billion, we immediately knew where we wanted to focus: on the biggest urban K–12 school systems in the country, the ones that largely educated the poor or minority students most in need.

Entering this area was, of course, an enormous risk. Many talented and intelligent men and women have attempted to reform education, and many have quit the effort because of the enormity of the problem, the lack of progress, and the system's resistance to change. Still, as you know, I never shy from an unreasonable goal. And as President Barack Obama's former chief of staff and now Chicago Mayor Rahm Emanuel once smartly told the *New York Times,* "Rule One: Never allow a crisis to go to waste. They are opportunities to do big things."

I think that's a good rule for everyone to keep in mind, no matter the type of crisis you find yourself confronting—be it a big new task or a bad year for your business, a shake-up in a field you want to enter, or a philanthropic cause you're about to tackle. When external forces are changing your world, think about what you can do to move with them, rather than reflexively hunkering down and refusing to change. Use crises as chances to rethink everything, question your assumptions, and start afresh. That's what we're trying to do in public education.

When we first started researching why progress wasn't happening in K–12 education in America, we discovered something interesting. A lot of proposals seemed to have merit, such as improving professional development, but the problem was deeper. These efforts alone wouldn't make enough of a difference because the systems themselves were broken. We needed an unreasonable solution.

Simply put, entrenched bureaucracies, policies, and practices are no longer set up in a way that helps teachers and students progress. Taxpayer resources often don't make it to the classroom. Teachers are left to fend for themselves without adequate real-time information about how well their students are learning, access to best practices, or time to collaborate. Because their pay and expectations are, in most cases, low, many talented Americans are dissuaded from entering the profession at all. Half of those who become teachers quit within their first five years. Ask any of your friends or family members who are teachers whether their central office is a help or a hindrance to them in the classroom. You can guess what they'll say.

How did urban school districts get here? I suspect the reason is because too few dared to ask the right "Why not?" question: Why not redesign these districts? It's a simple matter of reframing basic assumptions. Data show that the greatest positive outcomes for students happen when entire school systems are either redesigned or started anew. But too often school systems seem hesitant to apply or even explore the best practices of other governmental agencies, the nonprofit world, or business. Although the education systems are run by well-meaning people, those leaders' interests, training, and qualifications don't always adequately prepare them for managing an organization as enormous and hugely important as an urban school district.

Take my hometown. The budget for the Los Angeles Unified School District is $7 billion, the equivalent of a Fortune 500 company or a large federal government agency. Every decision every day—about how and where funds will be used, how policies will be set, how to run facilities, operations, human resources, and transportation—has an enormous impact. If these decisions are not closely attuned to student needs, too often school systems become preoccupied with jobs for adults rather than the futures of students. To solve the problems we face, entire school systems, including dozens or even hundreds of schools, must be transformed to empower teachers and students to succeed in the classroom.

This is why our foundation's goal is to help turn a tired government monopoly into a high-performing public enterprise that in fact serves the public. We identified the area where we could be particularly effective: improving management and finding talent. These skills are found in any high-performing organization—nonprofit, government, or private.

In determining how best to leverage our investment in improving America's public schools, we relied on the essential ingredient in any successful organization: smart people. I realized that if we could help identify or train effective school district leaders, they could give teachers the necessary resources and support. That's why we decided to focus our philanthropy on training and supporting superintendents—the CEOs of our country's 14,000-plus school districts—and other education leaders who can help many schools dramatically improve at once.

Nothing we have done to try to create change has been easy. One of the great things about our investments in scientific and medical research is the constant inspiration I derive from the scientific community's commitment to change. I've never met a scientist who didn't want to knock over the status quo. In education, by contrast, I've seen hundreds of millions of dollars and countless hours of effort spent defending and preserving what is clearly a broken system. Making any change requires a lot of unconventional wisdom, long-term thinking, innovation, and an unwavering focus on what matters most: helping America's students once again be the best in the world.

BIG GOALS AND BIG RESULTS

We launched The Broad Superintendents Academy in 2002 to train school district superintendents in how best to support teachers and students. We are proud that as of 2011, our graduates have taken on nearly 90 superintendent positions nationwide. Two-thirds of our graduates who have held their posts for at least three years are out-performing their peers in raising student achievement. We are also pleased that four Broad alumni have been named state superintendent of the year by their peers, and in 2012, one went on to be named the national superintendent of the year.

To help superintendents as they work to improve the basic functions of school systems, we created The Broad Residency to infuse management talent into K–12 public education. The two-year residency recruits successful early-career professionals with master's degrees and experience in business, law, and other public service sectors to work in public school systems, charter management organizations, or state and federal departments of education. More than 90 percent of Broad Residency alumni remain in public education after their first two years. Many are promoted rapidly and attain high levels of responsibility. Those who return to their original fields take with them a passion for education reform and become advocates for improving public education.

TAKING BIG RISKS MEANS GETTING BIG PUSHBACK

If your goals are large and public, you will face criticism. I know I have. I listen to it all, but I change my behavior based only on critiques that are valid. There is no reason to listen to criticism based on bias, resentment, or fear.

As soon as we started working in education, we faced a deluge of attacks, particularly online. Believe it or not, we pay attention. We pay less attention to name-calling and knee-jerk screeds, but we never ignore concerns rooted in logic.

When I'm not getting criticism for getting involved in public education as a concerned private individual, I'm usually being hammered for not doing enough. As venture philanthropists, we take far bigger risks than government organizations or older foundations, even if we share the same goal: To spur and sustain dramatic increases in academic achievement for students of all backgrounds.

As much as we hope our contributions will help catalyze large-scale change, education is a $600 billion industry. The $4 billion that goes into education philanthropy each year is a drop in the bucket. For something as important as the reinvention of our public education systems, entire communities must be accountable. We try to provide policymakers and the public with access to research, data, and best practices in education where we can, and we have supported local efforts where we think they will truly help students and teachers succeed. But elected officials, parents, teachers, taxpayers, and the media must join us to demand change.

The problem is immense. The solution must be big enough to match it. But there is good news. It is possible to challenge the status quo while honoring good teachers and defending public education. It is possible to encourage innovative, creative, and new solutions to tackle the challenges facing our public schools. And it is possible to provide all of our children with equal access to a free, quality public education, not just those lucky enough to live in an area with a great school, like I did 70 years ago.

Chapter 21

THE UNREASONABLENESS
OF ART AND ARTISTS

After Edye and I moved into our current home in Brentwood, we decided we wanted artwork as bold as the house itself. We knew exactly who to call: Richard Serra. He's America's greatest living sculptor, because he is brilliantly original, his work is always evolving, and he does things with steel that no one else would think possible.

I vividly recall the day Richard came over and walked around the yard, visualizing where the sculpture would go. His initial concept involved four 40-foot-tall steel columns. I pointed out that Edye and I live in earthquake country, which would make such a work unwise if not impossible. So Richard came up with a proposal that merely was unreasonable.

He wanted to stand four steel panels, each 15 feet high and 21 feet long, on the lawn and curve them into each other like a nest. Each steel panel would be 2 inches thick and weigh 15 tons. No place on the West Coast could handle that sort of job, so the panels would have to be fabricated at the Lukens Steel Company in Coatesville, Pennsylvania, and then shaped at the old General Dynamics plant in Rhode Island. General Dynamics was willing to take on the work to fill the hours when they weren't building nuclear submarines.

Then, because the panels were wider than any highway lane and taller than most overpasses, they would have to be trucked on four separate flatbed trucks across the country with multiple police escorts. When they arrived, we would have to rip out some trees and walls to install the piece. Because no helicopter could carry that weight, our steep driveway would have to be lined with steel plates and strengthened with concrete beams so that each piece could be put in place. I started to wonder if that was how the pyramids were built.

When Edye and I suggested to Richard that this sounded a bit too unreasonable—even for me—he assured us: "It's really no problem. Don't worry."

We gave Richard the go-ahead. His panels finally arrived around midnight the weekend before Thanksgiving. We got a phone call that a package was at the door, as if it were a Federal Express delivery. On the side of each panel, written in chalk, were the words "Not submarine work," just to be clear.

At one point, we reminded Richard there was no title for the work. Edye recalled what he had told us about the installation, and her wry humor came to the fore. She suggested, *No Problem*. The name stuck.

Why I Collect

More than one guest has taken a look at *No Problem* and asked, "What the heck is that?"

I had the same reaction when I first began looking at contemporary art. I didn't get it. People like Cy Twombly with his pale, repeated marks on canvas and Frank Stella with his complex metal works were posing provocative questions not only about the nature of art but also about perception itself. Of course, I didn't know all that at the time. I was experiencing what the art critic Robert Hughes called the shock of the new.

The first artwork we purchased was a drawing by Vincent Van Gogh. It was a nice, peaceful scene of two thatched huts. You didn't have to wonder at it, and it certainly wasn't jarring, but after several years I grew a little tired of it. I needed something that grabbed me—and that didn't have to be put in a drawer for six months out of the year to keep it from fading. I set up a trade so we could acquire a Robert Rauschenberg red painting, which remains in our home today and still is one of my favorite pieces.

I moved into contemporary art for a number of reasons. It was, in part, a homework-based decision. I knew that the best collections were generally built at the time the artists were alive. That way, the collection represents an era and the collector's personal taste. Your money also goes further when you're placing bets on the future.

Mostly, though, I decided to collect contemporary art because it moves me and it makes me think. It was risky because you never know whether an artist you support will maintain his or her reputation. Critical opinion, which drives markets, is subject to fashion. A drawing by Van Gogh is a safe bet—a Jeff Koons *Balloon Dog* less so.

I also enjoy meeting artists and watching them work. They're unlike anyone I meet in business. By definition, artists are "Why not?" thinkers. They do what no one else would think to do. They often work very hard without seeing great returns or receiving any particular acknowledgment in their lifetimes. They tackle, with brutal honesty, the politics and social issues of their times. They follow their vision no matter how strange it seems according to the conventional wisdom. I can relate to that. I wouldn't trade the opportunity to meet them and see them work for all the Van Goghs in the world.

By the early 1980s Edye and I had become such avid collectors of contemporary art that we started to run out of wall space in our home. But we wanted to continue collecting. We began to look for ways to share our collection with an audience far wider than our family and circle of friends. We hit on the idea of establishing a foundation that would function as a lending library for institutions, essentially creating a public collection.

Doing Homework—Even for an Avocation—Will Deepen Your Experience

Enjoyment and satisfaction increase with knowledge—even when it comes to hobbies.

Collecting contemporary art takes a lot of homework because you have to judge the work of a living person. When we consider buying an artwork, we think about where an artist fits in among his or her contemporaries and how the work would integrate into our collections. Most of all, we think about the work itself—how significant is it and how evocative? All of this research has enriched my life immeasurably and required me to use a different set of skills and a different part of my brain than I did in business. You should seek out a passion that allows you to do the same. It will enrich your life in ways business success simply can't.

In the 1980s we took major risks with the works we purchased. Edye and I spent a lot of time in New York's East Village, where we got to see work by up-and-comers like Keith Haring and Jean-Michel Basquiat, who once smoked pot in the bathroom of our house. The most exciting discovery of those years for me was photographer and artist Cindy Sherman. Edye and I weren't photography collectors, but I was fascinated by Cindy, who would make herself over into all sorts of characters and then photograph herself—an interesting twist on the traditional self-portrait. In 1982 we bought several early black-and-white photos of hers for $200 each from a show in the basement of the trendsetting gallery Metro Pictures on Mercer Street. They were from a series she calls *Untitled Film Stills*, and I wish we had bought every one of those photos. I still enjoy the theatricality of Cindy's works and the way they always surprise me. Today, we have the largest collection of her work in the world.

Sometimes we've been late to the game with an artist. In the mid-1990s, for example, a few years after I saw Andy Warhol's retrospective at the Museum of Modern Art, we began buying his art.

I didn't recognize the importance of his work until that show. Now we have a major group of his paintings in our personal art collection, including *Small Torn Campbell's Soup Can (Pepper Pot)*, which I bought for $11.7 million. Edye had wanted to buy a Warhol soup can print in the 1960s for $100 but didn't for fear I would think she was nuts—which I probably would have. About 40 years later, she thought I was the nutty one. We were at that auction together when I bought *Pepper Pot*, but I had bid so discreetly that she didn't realize I was the winner. After it was over, she whispered in my ear, "What idiot paid that much?"

In the end, whether you spend $500, $5,000, or $5 million, only one thing matters: You have to want to look at it. You have to love it. That's priceless.

PURSUING A PASSION SOMETIMES MEANS CASTING ASIDE YOUR BUSINESS SENSE

Jeff Koons is one of the artists to whose work I'm instinctually drawn. As we did with Cindy Sherman, Edye and I met Jeff in the 1980s in New York. I immediately thought he was brilliant. His background as a commodities trader was different from that of most other artists and piqued my interest. I found his art playful, fun to look at it, and, like Cindy's, bold and theatrical.

But in the early 1990s, the art market was going through a recession, just like the economy in general. Jeff was having a hard time selling works and had trouble getting an ambitious and groundbreaking series of his called *Celebration* off the ground. The most important sculpture of the series, *Balloon Dog*, would require $700,000 to fabricate, just for the first of four planned versions of the work.

I decided to do something I rarely do—pay in full for works that have not yet been fabricated. I entered into a $1 million contract to fund the fabrication of *Balloon Dog* and another sculpture from the same series. I did it because I believed in Jeff and his work.

As he began work on the project, however, it became clear that the fabrication costs of *Balloon Dog*—an oversized sculpture reminiscent of a childhood balloon animal but constructed from reflective stainless steel—would exceed the earlier estimates. The dealers wanted me to cover the cost overruns, which I might not have done in business. But art isn't business.

Nonetheless, I approached the situation as a negotiation with Jeff and his dealers. I immediately considered their incentives, which, fortunately, were aligned with mine: We all wanted to see completed works. In addition, the dealers wanted to sell at a strong price.

I suggested to Jeff that he increase the number of versions from four to five. For Jeff and his dealers, a fifth *Balloon Dog* would mean the sale of one more piece. Most collectors wouldn't actively encourage the creation of more versions of an artwork because that means their piece is less rare. But I wanted my Koons artwork, and I wanted to help Jeff's work take off again.

It worked. *Balloon Dog* was completed and became a very coveted piece. Our dramatic 12-foot-tall blue sculpture was shown as far away as the Guggenheim in Bilbao, Spain, and it most recently spent four years at The Broad Contemporary Art Museum at the Los Angeles County Museum of Art.

HOW NOT TO GET DISTRACTED BY YOUR PASSION

I don't like wasting time, so I got in the habit of working studio visits and museum trips into my business or philanthropic travel schedule. People often think it's strange how briskly I go through museums. Sure, I could stand in front of each piece and stare at it for a good long time. But that's not me. Usually I'm there to learn and apply my knowledge to our collections. As much as I would like to stay, I have to move on.

While I may dash through a museum, I do give myself time to take in artists' studios and art fairs in Miami, London, Venice, and Basel. The experience of an artist's studio is always inspiring and sometimes unusual. Some years ago, for instance, I dropped by British artist Damien Hirst's studio only to be handed a protective astronaut-like suit so I could watch him lower a shark's carcass into a tank of toxic chemicals. Although that's probably not everyone's cup of tea, I loved it. Browsing art fairs is just as enriching for me—it's exciting and intimate, and it lets me into a world I would never have known if I had stuck to business. Sometimes it's just plain fun.

Take the Art Basel fair in Switzerland in 2009, where I had the chance to give some art advice to an aspiring collector. I was walking through the fair with Edye when I saw a lot of cameras pointed at some guy wearing a hat and sunglasses even though we were inside. I had no idea who he was, but I've never been one to resist a camera. I walked right up to him and looked at the artwork he was contemplating—a 9-foot-long Neo Rauch painting of a race track, *Etappe*. Our foundation has a fair number of works by Rauch, a native of East Germany whose work combines the seemingly contradictory influences of socialist realism and surrealism. We discussed the work and the artist, and I said it was a good piece and we would probably buy it if he didn't. He ended up purchasing the work. After I had walked away, Edye finally told me who I had been talking to: Brad Pitt. He has a good eye.

A Passion Is Not a License to Spend

Just as I don't spend more time than I can spare on art, I don't spend more money than necessary either. I always look to leverage what I do spend.

One of my attempts to do that has entered art world folklore. In 1995 I purchased a classic painting from Roy Lichtenstein's high pop period titled *I . . . I'm Sorry*. I had first seen the painting on the wall of dealer Holly Solomon's New York living room. It depicted a comic-book blond—actually, it was supposed to be Holly herself—weeping a lone tear and apologizing in a speech bubble. I liked it on first sight, but it would be 15 years until I finally acquired it.

As I walked into Sotheby's auction room that day and was given a paddle, I asked if it was true that they accepted credit cards. They did. As it happens, I had a high-credit-limit American Express card that gave me a frequent flyer mile for every dollar I put on it. I bought the Lichtenstein for $2.5 million—which I knew was a fair price because other Lichtensteins of that period were selling for a lot more—and I put the purchase on my card.

It caused quite a ruckus. Sotheby's had to negotiate down the transaction fee with American Express. People wondered what I would do with that many frequent flyer miles—actually, I donated them to students at CalArts. The real reason for charging the purchase, which shouldn't surprise you by now, was the interest. Rather than handing over $2.5 million up front, I could keep my money invested, earn my usual high return, and pay for the piece when my AmEx bill came due, a little more than a month later.

When the next season's sales rolled around, Sotheby's auctioneer called me out and got a big laugh from the crowd: "We no longer take credit cards . . . Eli."

For Even Greater Rewards, Share What You Love

No matter what your pursuit, the most fulfilling part is sharing it with others. You wouldn't want to cook gourmet meals just for yourself or perform on the piano only in private.

But art can be different. A lot of collectors in the world want to buy an artwork just so they can look at it or say they own it. Edye and I have never felt that way. If we buy a work, it's because we want a lot of people to be able to see it. When The Broad Contemporary Art Museum opened at the Los Angeles County Museum of Art, I told Director Michael Govan he could borrow any works from our collections, including those hanging in our house. He came in and practically stripped the walls, and we were delighted.

Although The Broad Art Foundation has made more than 8,000 loans to nearly 500 museums since 1984, there still was the question of what Edye and I would do with our personal art collection after we passed away. We had a few options: split it up between a few museums, create a small gallery but continue primarily as a lending library, or build our own museum. Most museums keep the bulk of their art in storage, which we didn't want to happen to the pieces in our collections. A small gallery, even with an aggressive lending policy, would have the same effect—hiding most of our collections from public view. And as they kept growing to nearly 2,000 works, we realized no museum could ever show more than a few of our works at a time.

Building a museum was the most challenging option but also the most rewarding. The Broad will allow our collections to stay whole and be accessible to the greatest number of people in Los Angeles and in museums worldwide. With the Museum of Contemporary Art across the street, our museum will make downtown Los Angeles a nexus for contemporary art and jump-start further development in the area. It also will serve as the headquarters of The Broad Art Foundation's lending library, making sure that all our art does what it was made to do: bring beauty, inspiration, and the shock of the new to as many people as possible.

Chapter 22

REFLECTIONS AND SECOND THOUGHTS

In the preceding pages, I've shared with you some of the mental habits and day-to-day practices that I believe have helped me succeed over the past six decades across four careers. These principles and practices grow out of a mind-set most people would regard as unreasonable. But to the extent you make this mind-set yours, you can achieve more than you ever thought possible. Demand the unreasonable of yourself and you will exceed everyone's expectations, not least your own.

The unreasonable life is lived with confidence, decisiveness, and drive, but it does not guarantee happiness. Success cannot inoculate you against difficult times. Every life brings regret, tragedy, and crisis—the moments that test our ability to cope. My life, however rich in experience and material rewards it may outwardly appear, is no exception.

I take pride in my achievements but I recognize my mistakes. I know what I would like my legacy to be, but I also know I can't control what others will make of it. At the very least, I hope that what I have done will survive me and continue improving the lives of others long after mine has ended.

MY PARENTS' UNINTENTIONAL GIFT

Looking back, I can see that my parents laid the foundation of my unreasonable life by giving me unusual independence at an early age. They both came from big families and, growing up in the Bronx, I had a lot of cousins and aunts and uncles around me on weekends. My closest friends were my cousin Rube, who lived near us, and—later— my pal Burt Binder, a high school classmate with whom I remained close until he passed away a few years ago.

But mostly, I was alone. I had no siblings. Between the ages of 7 and 14, I had no one I really could call a close friend. My parents both worked long hours. In the free time he had, my father usually hung out with friends. My mother worked late into the night keeping his books.

Being so solitary at a young age shaped me into the man I am today. I learned to think and make decisions independently long before most people do. I never had to seek anyone's approval, so I didn't develop the habit of wanting it. I learned to be comfortable with silence. I acquired the attitudes that many people would later find unreasonable—a thick skin and a laser focus. Many people would consider a solitary childhood sad, perhaps even a misfortune. But for me it became a school of opportunity—and I made the most of it.

MY SONS AND MY CHOICE—ON THAT ELUSIVE WORK-LIFE BALANCE

My father worked hard to give me the childhood I had, but he wasn't often a part of it. He usually filled his leisure hours with friends. But he still tried to spend time with me when he could. He earned enough money to take us on vacations in the winter. He took me to political rallies. We were in the car together when we heard on the radio that Pearl Harbor had been attacked. And throughout my adult years, I knew he was deeply proud of me. He carried an early newspaper article about Kaufman and Broad in his wallet until his last day.

I tried to do more for my sons than my father could do for me. I had always wanted two children so that they would have each other's company in addition to mine. Jeffrey and Gary were born in 1956 and 1959, respectively. I taught them how to ride bikes, fly kites, and play chess. I tried to help Jeffrey learn to read and overcome his dyslexia, a condition with which I had struggled as a kid. But it was Edye who spent long hours doing visual training exercises with him. I went to Gary's baseball games when my hours allowed. He was an impressive athlete, something I never had been. I insisted on having dinner as a family in the evenings whenever I got off work. But I confess: I was serious, focused, demanding, and not much fun. I took the boys with me to tour subdivisions, and now I realize that's not exactly how kids want to spend their weekends.

I missed too many moments, and I regret it. I know it from watching the way other parents are with their children. Jeffrey's and Gary's childhoods coincided with the years of expansion at Kaufman and Broad. We moved once to Arizona when they were very young and again to Los Angeles. I traveled twice a month to our other offices, particularly when we were opening and trying to master new markets, as we did throughout the 1960s and 1970s. Time with my sons was precious but unfortunately rare.

Lines from a poem by William Butler Yeats, "The Choice," have always given me some small solace when I reflect on my family life:

> The intellect of man is forced to choose
> perfection of the life, or of the work.

By now, you know which I chose. Although I am proud of my accomplishments, I sometimes wonder whether I should have chosen differently.

But perhaps Yeats's choice is too stark. If I could do it again, I would have tried to find perfection in a balance between the two, as I hope you will try to do. An unreasonable life can take you far in your career, but sometimes it can take you too far from home.

Don't Let Others Define Your Failures or Your Successes

No matter the sort of life you choose to lead, you will wonder if you chose correctly. Whatever choices you make about life, work, or the balance between them, others will second-guess or even criticize you.

My family and I, thankfully, have kept much of our privacy. But my work is public, and along with respect and accolades, I have faced much criticism.

As I have told you, I ignore criticism that is merely carping, but I do accept it when it makes sense. It's important to understand the events you regard as failures—but never let other people decide what they are. I know when I fell short in my career. There were failed deals and negotiations and purchases. There were relationships that went dry. And there were what I consider the true missteps. As a young accountant, I was good at numbers but bad at being decorous with the higher-ups. As a homebuilder, I chose the wrong time to leave my company in someone else's hands, and I also made perhaps the biggest mistake of my business life.

In 1966 Kaufman and Broad formed Nation Wide Cablevision. This early entry into the cable industry represented a very shrewd move on our part—almost. In 1972 our three main businesses—homebuilding, life insurance, and cable—all demanded a great deal of capital, so we sold Nation Wide to Tele-Communications, Inc. (TCI) for a 15 percent share of TCI, which we immediately cashed in for $23.5 million. It felt like a coup at the time because we had shed a business that we knew couldn't grow without heavy spending on technology and infrastructure. TCI, however, went on to become the country's largest cable provider. It was later acquired by AT&T and then sold to Comcast. Comcast today is worth $73 billion—something utterly unimaginable when we got out of the cable business. I should have sold the homebuilding company and kept cable.

Then there are the moments that are disappointments rather than clear failures. One of the most difficult periods in my business career, in fact, occurred through no fault of my own. At SunAmerica, we protected our customers' savings by refusing to bet the farm on junk bonds and other risky investments. But a lot of other insurers did not take the same precautions. Our company fell under regulatory scrutiny simply because we were in the same business. Trying to assure regulators that our books were clean of high-risk investments was one of the more stressful experiences of my life. We managed to convince them after a series of meetings and after promising to adopt stricter regulations for ourselves.

Finally, in philanthropy, no matter how proud I am of our foundations' work in education, I am overwhelmed by how much remains to be done. We can't possibly restore America's public schools to greatness without a unified call from the public. Everyone has to work together to fix the system so that teachers and students have the support they need to succeed.

My Proudest Moments—They May Not Be What You Think

Just as it is important to know your failures, it's critical to be clear about what you consider your successes. I'm proud of making life better for people by building affordable homes for families, creating secure futures for retirees, generating high-performing returns for shareholders and employees, boosting the education of American children, improving the health of people around the globe, and broadening the perspective of museum-goers with the chance to appreciate the art of their own time.

I've always been driven to build, to create, to challenge the status quo. But I don't define myself by my bank account. That's why I'm particularly proud that the companies I created were known as places that treated employees, customers, vendors, and competitors fairly and conducted their business with integrity under my watch.

I'm even prouder of the early acquisitions and decisions that created SunAmerica than the billions we made merging it with AIG. If you're an entrepreneur, you have to value the rush you get from the building, not the paycheck—otherwise, the work is just too hard and the sacrifices too great.

I'm proud that in 1954 I became the youngest certified public accountant in Michigan. If you've ever read a long journalistic profile of me, you'll probably recall that fact. That's because I keep mentioning it to reporters. After being a fairly mediocre student my whole life, I was glad to learn, at age 20, that I actually could excel at something. I'm happy to note, though, that in 2010, that distinction passed to Bradley Brennan, a University of Michigan–Dearborn graduate who beat my record by four months.

I could choose to take pride in Kaufman and Broad's 100,000th house in 1977—and I am proud of that—but I'm more pleased with having gone public in 1961 on the American Stock Exchange and then becoming the first homebuilder listed on the New York Stock Exchange in 1969. I was only 28 at the time of the first listing, and young entrepreneurs were not quite the hot investment prospects they would become in the era of Silicon Valley.

Even more than creating a publicly traded company, I am proud simply of having started a business that got off the ground. In the end, nothing else matters more. If you've ever pulled it off, be proud of yourself. If you're trying to do it, set your goals high but take pride in the most essential success of simply beginning. As you go, always define success for yourself, not by someone else's criteria. Don't judge yourself on awards and bank balances or strive for some magical number of fans, friends, or followers, thinking your work is done if you just "make it." As long as you're around, your work—whether that's your job, your family, your philanthropy, or your pursuit of knowledge—is never done.

I HOPE MY GREATEST ACHIEVEMENT IS YET TO COME

I take to heart the idea that my work is never done. That's why I'm most proud of my fourth career: philanthropy. People often assume that the wealthy engage in philanthropy out of guilt. That might have been true for Andrew Carnegie, whose career in business involved some deplorable incidents. But for most of this generation of philanthropists, it is a matter of applying skills learned from what we've done best—running a business—to the most pressing problems of our time. It's not about guilt. It's about obligation—the duties of decency and solidarity that each of us owes this country.

I'm also proud of my work on behalf of Los Angeles. Critics have predicted the demise of Los Angeles since it was a dusty pueblo alongside an unreliable river, but my favorite city survives and thrives. To anyone who fears for its future, I reply that Los Angeles has become one of four major cultural capitals of the world, and Hollywood movies still enchant and enthrall the world more than any other artistic product from anywhere. Downtown L.A. has a vibrancy that rivals many other American cities and that will only increase with development on Grand Avenue. Industries that are key to the future of our country, like technology, biotech, and energy, are expanding in Los Angeles. However difficult the recession is, I have confidence in the long-term future of our city and country.

My family came to America from a country that ultimately would murder its Jews. Here they found more than safety. They found work and opportunity and the security to participate in politics and to speak their beloved Yiddish to one another in their home. I was educated in free public schools and in a great university whose costs were modest enough that even a son of lower-middle-class parents could easily meet them.

In Los Angeles I found perhaps the world's greatest meritocracy— a city that apportions success according to your own efforts and not according to family, background, or class. In my working lifetime here, I've happily watched as even this city's old barriers built on race, ethnicity, gender, and sexual orientation have continued to fall away.

Obviously, you want to give back to a place like that. I'm very proud of my role in establishing the Museum of Contemporary Art and in helping raise the money to build Disney Hall. I'm honored to have launched well-planned rather than piecemeal development downtown, secured funding for a park on Grand Avenue, and seeded medical research at Caltech, USC, UCLA, and UC San Francisco. I also expect that The Broad will one day be a respected contemporary art museum, patronized as faithfully as the Frick, the Morgan Library, and the Norton Simon.

The philanthropic work of our foundations, although based in Los Angeles, reaches far beyond the city's boundaries. In education—certainly the most difficult of our philanthropic efforts—we have invested across the country in smart people and institutions that will keep challenging the status quo. We have no choice but to radically transform our schools or else be surpassed by other countries not only in educational achievement but also in economic growth and innovation. The solutions to the serious problems that face our world—a recessionary economic environment, unsustainable energy consumption, skyrocketing health care costs—start with education. Moreover, we have no more right to starve our children of knowledge and the ability to apply it than we do to starve them of food.

In medicine, I know we are laying the foundation for ground-breaking understanding of disease, treatment, and hopefully prevention. Of all we have done over the past six decades, the effort I am most proud of is the creation of The Broad Institute. It is already first in the world in genomics. We have a brilliant leader in Eric Lander, large federal grants, and institutional support from two of the best universities in the world, Harvard and MIT. We have 1,900 gifted young scientists and a board that includes the presidents of Harvard and MIT, Genentech Chairman Art Levinson, and Lou Gerstner, the former CEO of IBM. The biomedical investments of The Broad Foundations will improve the lives of many more people than my businesses could ever reach and for many more years.

Medicine was something I knew nothing about. But when Edye and I visited Eric Lander's lab in Cambridge, we got a feel for it and we saw the raw talent in the room. As usual, I was focused on the practical—what could we do and how much it would cost. Edye, though, has a quicker and just as astute instinct when it comes to people. She caught on fast to Eric, who is an accomplished communicator. We weren't even back in Los Angeles before she started to say, "We should give him all our money."

THE BEST MOVE I EVER MADE

I began this book by telling you that the one constant throughout my career has been the paperweight Edye gave me with the quote from George Bernard Shaw. But the real constant in my life is, of course, Edye.

We have been married for almost 58 years. She realized early to how unreasonable I am, and although she doesn't always like it, she loves and understands me. She brings me back down to earth when I need it and pulls me out of the weeds when I wander. She listens to me and advises me. She teaches me about the best things in life: art, companionship, and family. I am fond of saying that, while a lot of people don't love me, everyone loves Edye. It's true. Everyone does, me most of all.

We had to learn, sometimes, to live around each other. I agreed to forgo mortgages, to stay in the same Los Angeles neighborhood for decades, and to not let my mind wander too far during certain family gatherings. She gives me a pass on operas and symphonies, which I've rarely attended, but I encourage her to go with her friends. Mostly she allows me to be as I am—always working, always restless, but always anchored.

We have not always had an easy road and have had our rough patches. Our most difficult trial was decades ago. Edye had a serious medical crisis when she was only 20 years old. No matter that it grows more distant with each passing day, no matter that she and I are healthy in our late 70s, thinking about that time still tears me apart. I spent the months when she was sick trying my hardest and often nearly failing simply to live through each day.

I am grateful for every day we've had together since, for those dark days that taught me what really matters, and for the days before, when I was just barely hanging on to my job, when I was only an artlessly unreasonable nobody Edye loved.

Back then, when I first began talking about starting a business, I remember her joking that I had to do it and I had to be good at it because she didn't know how to cook. We ate out all the time or at our parents' houses. One of the first meals we ate in our own place—a tiny rented home—was not your usual dinner. Edye had managed to make a Pillsbury chocolate cake by following the recipe on the box. I came home from my job at a small accounting firm, Goldman and Golman, to the wonderful smell of baking. We split the cake down the middle, and we each ate half. It remains one of the best meals I've ever had.

I have made poor choices, in business, in my personal life, and in the way I balanced those two. But I made one brilliant choice that outshines everything else I've done: I asked Edye to marry me. Who you spend your life with—much more so than how you choose to spend it—is the most important decision you can make. Do it right. That's the best advice I can give you.

Appendix

ELI BROAD CAREER HIGHLIGHTS

CURRENT ACTIVITIES

The Broad Foundations; Founder
The Eli and Edythe L. Broad Foundation	1967–
The Broad Art Foundation	1984–

BUSINESS CAREER

Certified Public Accountant	1954–1956
Detroit Institute of Technology, Assistant Professor	1956
KB Home (formerly Kaufman and Broad Home Corporation); (NYSE: KBH)	
Cofounder, Chairman and CEO	1957–1989
Chairman	1989–1993
Chairman of Executive Committee	1993–1995
SunAmerica Inc. (formerly NYSE: SAI)	
Founder, Chairman and CEO	1989–2000
Founder and Chairman	2001–2005
AIG Retirement Services, Inc. (NYSE: AIG)	
Chairman	1999–2005

EDUCATION

Central High School, Detroit, Michigan; graduated	1951
Michigan State University; graduated cum laude	1954
Bachelor of Arts: major Accounting, minor Economics	

PROFESSIONAL

Beta Alpha Psi, Accounting Honorary	1953
Certified Public Accountant, Michigan	1956

CIVIC ACTIVITIES

Center for the Study of the Presidency	
Board of Trustees	2007–
Smithsonian Institution, Board of Regents	2004–2009
Grand Avenue Committee	
Chair	2001–2007
Co-Vice Chair	2007–2009
Americans for Gun Safety, Board of Advisors	2001–
Asia Society, Board of Trustees	1999–2004
Los Angeles Police Foundation	
Founding Board Member	1998–2002
Advisory Board	2003–
Walt Disney Concert Hall	
Board of Directors	1998–2006
Oversight Board of Directors, Chairman	1997–1998
Campaign, Cochair	1997–1998
Los Angeles Global Forum, Chairman	1995
The Music Center of Los Angeles County	
Honorary Governor	1998–
Board of Governors	1996–1998
Board of Overseers	1991–1992
D.A.R.E. America	
Honorary Member of the Board of Directors	1995–
Board of Directors	1989–1995
Los Angeles World Affairs Council	
Lifetime Director	2004–
Chairman of Executive Committee	1997–1999

Chairman	1994–1997
Board of Directors	1988–2003
Los Angeles Business Journal, Advisory Board	1986–1988
Town Hall of California, Advisory Council	1985–1987
Boy Scouts of America, Advisory Board	1982–1985
Los Angeles Area Chamber of Commerce	
Board of Directors	1978–1979
YMCA, Los Angeles, Board of Directors	1975–1978
United Way, Los Angeles	
Alexis de Tocqueville Society	1989
Loaned Executive Campaign, Chairman	1980–1981
Board of Directors	1972–1974
National Brotherhood of Christians and Jews	
Board of Directors	1971–1976
City of Hope, Board of Directors, Executive Committee	1968–1978

EDUCATIONAL ACTIVITIES

Teach for America, Board of Directors	2003–2004
EdVoice	
Cochair	2008–
Board of Directors	2001–
Los Angeles Unified School District, Superintendent	
Search Committee	2000
University of Southern California, Keck School of	
Medicine	
Board of Overseers	1999–
The Eli and Edythe Broad Foundation, Founder and	
Trustee	1999–
Governor-Elect's Education Transition Task Force,	
California	1998
Children's Scholarship Fund, National Board of Advisors	1998–
California Institute of Technology	
Life Trustee	2007–

Senior Trustee	2005–2007
Board of Trustees	1993–2005
American Council on Education, Business-Higher	
Education Forum	1993–1995
California State University	
Trustee Emeritus	1982–
Board of Trustees	1978–1982
Board of Trustees, Vice Chairman	1979–1980
The Claremont Colleges, Claremont, California	
Executive Committee, Board of Fellows	1974–1979
Institute of International Education, Board of Directors	1973–1979
Haifa University, Board of Trustees	1972–1980
Windward School, Santa Monica, California	
Founding Trustee	1972–1977
University of California, Los Angeles	
School of the Arts and Architecture:	
Board of Visitors, Executive Committee	1997–
Board of Visitors, Cochairman	1995–1997
UCLA Foundation, Board of Governors	1997–1998
UCLA Foundation, Board of Trustees	1986–1996
Graduate School of Management, Visiting Committee	1972–1990
Pitzer College, Claremont, California	
Life Trustee	1982–
Board of Trustees	1970–1982
Chairman, Board of Trustees	1973–1979

ART ACTIVITIES

Future Generation Art Prize, Board member	2009–
Smithsonian Institution, Board of Regents	2004–2009
Museum of Modern Art, New York	
Life Trustee	2009–
Board of Trustees	2004–2009
Metropolitan Museum of Art, Chairman's Council	2003–

Exhibition: "Jasper Johns to Jeff Koons: Four Decades
of Art from The Broad Collections"
Los Angeles County Museum of Art; Corcoran
Gallery, Washington, D.C.; Museum of Fine Arts,
Boston; Guggenheim Museum, Bilbao, Spain   2001–2003

Museum of Photographic Arts, International Advisory
Board, Founding Chairman   1998–

American Friends of The Israel Museum, National
Committee   1995–

Exhibition: "The Assertive Image: Artists of the 80s
from the Eli Broad Family Foundation"
UCLA/Armand Hammer Museum of Art and
Cultural Center   1994

UCLA/Armand Hammer Museum of Art and Cultural
Center, Board of Directors   1994–1999

Guggenheim Museum, International Directors
Council   1993–1998

Harvard University Art Museums
Committee to Visit the Art Museums   1998–2004
Collections Committee and Contemporary Art
Subcommittee   1992

Exhibition: "Compassion and Protest: Recent Social and
Political Art from the Eli Broad Family Foundation
Collection"
San Jose Museum of Art   1991

The American Federation of Arts, Board
of Trustees   1988–1991

Whitney Museum, New York, Painting and Sculpture
Committee   1987–1989

Exhibition: "Reflections: Art of the Eighties, Selections
from the Collection of The Eli Broad Family
Foundation"
University of Iowa Museum of Art   1987

Exhibition: "Selections from The Eli Broad Collection/
  American Art of the 1980s"
  Phoenix Art Museum   1986
High Museum of Art, Atlanta, Georgia
  National Advisory Council   1986–1988
Archives of American Art, Smithsonian Institution,
  Board of Trustees   1985–1998
Baltimore Museum of Art, National Trustee   1985–1991
The Broad Art Foundation, Founder and Trustee   1984–
University of Southern California, Friends of Fine Arts 1982–1988
The Museum of Contemporary Art, Los Angeles
  Life Trustee   2004–
  Board of Trustees   1980–1993
  Founding Chairman   1980–1984
Fellows of Contemporary Art   1980–1989
Maeght Foundation, St. Paul de Vence, France   1975–1980
Los Angeles County Museum of Art
  Life Trustee   2008–
  Board of Trustees and Executive Committee   1995–2008
  Acquisitions Committee   1978–1981
  Contemporary Art Council   1973–1979
Business Committee for the Arts
  Advisory Committee for "From Workplaces to Public
  Spaces: Gifting Art from Business Collections to
  Public Institutions"   2006–
  Member   1972–1990,
                                                        1994–
  Board of Directors   2001–2003

BUSINESS ACTIVITIES

American International Group, Board of Directors   1999–2003
Los Angeles Business Advisors, Board of Directors   1997–2004

Sacramento Kings and ARCO Arena, Co-owner and Cochairman	1992–1999
The Advest Group, Inc. (NYSE), Board of Directors	1989–1990
Placer Ranch, Inc., Sacramento, California; President	1988–
California Business Roundtable	1986–2000
Finance and Development Inc., Paris, France, Board of Directors	1982–1984
National Energy Foundation, Board of Directors	1979–1986
Citibank, New York, Real Estate Advisory Board	1976–1981
Verex Corporation (NYSE), Board of Directors	1973–1980
Federal National Mortgage Association (NYSE)	
Board of Directors	1984–1995
Executive Committee Advisory Board	1972–1973
Council of Housing Producers, Co-Founder	1968

GOVERNMENTAL AND POLITICAL ACTIVITIES

Think Long Committee	2010–
Clinton Global Initiative, Participant	2006–
State of California, Governor-Elect's Transition Team, Member	2003
Democratic National Convention, Host Committee, Chairman	2000
State of California, Business, Transportation and Housing Agency, Commission on Building for the 21st Century	1999–2001
California Senate Special Committee on Local Government Investments Board of Advisors, Chairman	1994–1995
Mayor's Special Advisory Committee on Fiscal Administration, Los Angeles	1993–1994
Democratic National Committee Victory Fund, Trustee	1988, 1992, 1996

Mayor's Housing Policy Committee,
  Los Angeles, Chairman   1974–1975
State Economic Summit Conference, Delegate
  and Speaker   1974
Federal Economic Summit Conference,
  Delegate and Speaker   1974
California Non-Partisan Voter Registration
  Foundation, President   1971–1972
National Industrial Pollution Control Council   1970–1973
Democratic National Convention, Delegate   1968
Alan Cranston Senatorial Campaign
  State Chairman   1968

PHILANTHROPIC ACTIVITIES

The Broad Art Foundation
The Broad Medical Research Program
The Eli and Edythe Broad Foundation
California Institute of the Arts, The Eli and Edythe Broad Studios
California Institute of Technology, The Broad Center for the
  Biological Sciences
California Institute of Technology, Broad Fellows Program in
  Brain Circuitry
California Institute of Technology, University of California, Los
  Angeles, Joint Center for Translational Medicine
Cedars-Sinai Medical Center Women's Heart Center, The Edythe
  L. Broad Cardiology Research Fellowship
The Giving Pledge
LA Opera, Der Ring des Nibelungen
Los Angeles County Museum of Art, The Broad Contemporary Art
  Museum
Massachusetts Institute of Technology, Harvard University,
  Whitehead Institute, Eli and Edythe L. Broad Institute

Michigan State University, The Eli Broad College of Business and
The Eli Broad Graduate School of Management
Michigan State University, The Eli and Edythe Broad Art Museum
The Museum of Contemporary Art, Los Angeles, Founder and
Leadership Donor
The Music Center of Los Angeles County, Founder
Pitzer College, Edythe and Eli Broad Center and Broad Hall
Santa Monica Performing Arts Center, The Eli and Edythe Broad
Stage, The Edye Second Space
United Jewish Welfare Federation
United Way, Alexis de Tocqueville Society
University of California, Los Angeles, Eli and Edythe Broad
Art Center
University of California, Los Angeles, The Eli and Edythe Broad
Center of Regenerative Medicine and Stem Cell Research
University of California, San Francisco, The Eli and Edythe Broad
Center of Regeneration Medicine and Stem Cell Research
University of California, Santa Barbara, Gevirtz Graduate School of
Education Koegel Autism Center, The Eli and Edythe L. Broad
Center for Asperger Research
University of Southern California, Keck School of Medicine, The
Eli and Edythe Broad CIRM Center for Regenerative Medicine
and Stem Cell Research
Walt Disney Concert Hall, Los Angeles, Leadership Donor

HONORS AND RECOGNITION

College Art Association, Centennial Award for
Patronage and Philanthropic Support of the Arts   2012
The Edmund G. "Pat" Brown Institute of Public Affairs,
Pat Brown Lifetime Legacy Award   2011
Alfalfa Club   2010
KIPP Giving Tree Award   2010

United States Artists, Gala Honoree	2009
Museum of Modern Art, David Rockefeller Award	2009
Carnegie Medal of Philanthropy	2007
Pepperdine University Graziadio School of Business and Management Honorary Doctorate of Law	2007
American Gastroenterological Association Outstanding Service Award	2007
University of California, Los Angeles Medal	2006
Louise T. Blouin Foundation Award	2006
Los Angeles Business Journal, Business Person of the Year Award	2005
Young Audiences, Arts for Learning, Gala Honoree	2005
American Institute of Architects Los Angeles Chapter, Service to the Community Award	2005
Americans for the Arts, Frederick R. Weisman Award for Philanthropy in the Arts	2005
Archives of American Art, Smithsonian Institution, Archives of American Art Medal	2004
American Society for Public Administration Los Angeles Metropolitan Chapter, Earl Warren Outstanding Public Service Award	2004
Los Angeles Chamber of Commerce, Civic Medal of Honor	2004
Israel Philharmonic Orchestra, Honoree	2003
United Friends of the Children, Brass Ring Award	2003
Los Angeles County Economic Development Corporation, Eddy Award	2002
Michigan State University, Honorary Degree of Doctor of Humanities	2002
United Way, The Alexis de Tocqueville Award	2002
University of California, Los Angeles, The Anderson School, Exemplary Leadership in Management Award	2002
Teach for America, Educational Leadership Award	2001

American Academy of Arts and Sciences, Fellow	2001
University of Southern California, School of Policy, Planning, and Development, The Julius Award	2001
Southwestern University, School of Law, Honorary Degree of Doctor of Laws	2000
Occidental College, Founders Award	2000
California Institute of the Arts, Trustees Award	2000
Asia Society of Southern California, Chairman's Award	2000
Southern California Leadership Network, Southern California Leader of the Year	1999
Los Angeles Chamber of Commerce, Lifetime Achievement Award	1999
KCET, Visionary Award	1999
Central City Association, Heart of the City Award	1999
Harvard Business School Association of Southern California, Business Statesman of the Year	1999
Downtown Breakfast Club, Rose Award for Business Leadership	1999
California State Forum, Forum Award	1998
The Music Center of Los Angeles County, L.A. Alive!, Honoree	1998
Orange County Museum of Art, Art of Dining XI, Honors Award	1998
Financial World Magazine, CEO of the Year, Finance	1998
Greater Los Angeles African American Chamber of Commerce, Community Service Award	1998
Los Angeles Business Journal, Leadership Award	1998
Bet Tzedek, The House of Justice, Distinguished Community Service and Leadership Award	1998
Los Angeles Headquarters Association, Community Service Award	1998
Business Committee for the Arts, Leadership Award	1997

The Museum of Contemporary Art, Gala and Tribute
Celebration, Honoree   1997
Los Angeles Convention and Visitors Bureau, Los
Amigos de Los Angeles Award   1997
University of Southern California, Lusk Center for Real
Estate Development, Hall of Fame   1996
Republic of France, Chevalier in the National Order of
the Legion of Honor   1994
Los Angeles Arts Council, Honors Award, Visual Arts   1989
Coro Foundation, Public Affairs Award   1987
Anti-Defamation League of B'nai B'rith, American
Heritage Award   1984
NAACP, ACT-SO Award   1982
Federation of Labor, AFL-CIO, Los Angeles, Labor's
Award of Honor for Community Services to the Arts   1982
National Housing Conference, Housing Man of the
Year Award   1979
National Conference of Christians and Jews,
Humanitarian Award   1977
American Academy of Achievement   1971, 1998
Michigan State University, Distinguished Alumni
Award   1968
Professional Builder Magazine, Builder of the Year
Award   1967
City of Hope, Man of the Year Award   1965
Listed in: Who's Who in the World, in America, in the
West, in Business and Finance

INDEX

Note: Photographs and associated captions are indicated by an italicized *I* and page number.